INCREDIBLE COMICS

with TOM NGUYEN

THE ULTIMATE GUIDE TO CREATING KICK-ASS COMIC ART

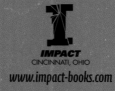

IMPACT
CINCINNATI, OHIO
www.impact-books.com

METRIC CONVERSION CHART

To convert	to	multiply by
Inches	Centimeters	2.54
Centimeters	Inches	0.4
Feet	Centimeters	30.5
Centimeters	Feet	0.03
Yards	Meters	0.9
Meters	Yards	1.1

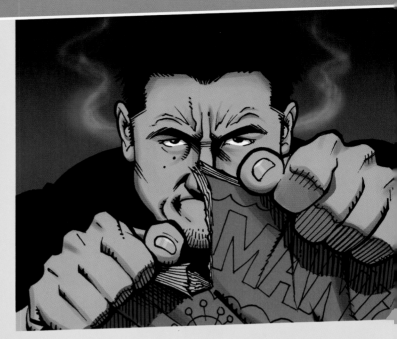

Incredible Comics With Tom Nguyen. Copyright © 2007 by Tom Nguyen. Manufactured in China. All rights reserved. No part of this book may be reproduced in any form or by any electronic or mechanical means including information storage and retrieval systems without permission in writing from the publisher, except by a reviewer who may quote brief passages in a review. Published by North Light Books, an imprint of F+W Publications, Inc., 4700 East Galbraith Road, Cincinnati, Ohio, 45236. (800) 289-0963. First Edition.

fw
F+W PUBLICATIONS, INC.

Other fine North Light Books are available from your local bookstore, art supply store or direct from the publisher at www.fwbookstore.com.

11 10 09 08 07   5 4 3 2 1

DISTRIBUTED IN CANADA BY FRASER DIRECT
100 Armstrong Avenue
Georgetown, ON, Canada L7G 5S4
Tel: (905) 877-4411

DISTRIBUTED IN THE U.K. AND EUROPE BY DAVID & CHARLES
Brunel House, Newton Abbot, Devon, TQ12 4PU, England
Tel: (+44) 1626 323200, Fax: (+44) 1626 323319
Email: postmaster@davidandcharles.co.uk

DISTRIBUTED IN AUSTRALIA BY CAPRICORN LINK
P.O. Box 704, S. Windsor NSW, 2756 Australia
Tel: (02) 4577-3555

Library of Congress Cataloging in Publication Data
Nguyen, Tom
  Incredible comics with Tom Nguyen : the ultimate guide to creating kick-ass comic art / by Tom Nguyen.
      p. cm.
  Includes index.
  ISBN-13: 978-1-58180-946-6 (pbk. : alk. paper)
  ISBN-10: 1-58180-946-8 (pbk. : alk. paper)
  1. Comic books, strips, etc.--Technique. 2. Cartooning--Technique. I. Title.
  NC1764.N48 2007
  741.5'1--dc22   2007005774

Edited by Jeffrey Blocksidge
Designed by Wendy Dunning
Production coordinated by Matt Wagner

ABOUT THE AUTHOR

Tom was born in 1976 in Minneapolis, Minnesota, a year after his parents, Thao and Thien, immigrated to the U.S. from South Vietnam. Growing up as the oldest of three children, he always had a knack for drawing and drew his favorite cartoon and comic book characters in his spare time. In his teen years, Tom switched his attention to portraiture, but his love for comic book art never went away.

Throughout high school, Tom made his side money drawing live airbrushed caricatures at Valleyfair theme park and the Mall of America in Minnesota. In 1996 he broke into the world of professional comics at age 19 as an inker for DC Comics, working with Doug Mahnke on the ill-fated title, *Major Bummer*. Since then, his work has branched out into other huge titles such as *Superman: The Man of Steel*, *Batman* and *JLA* among others.

While doing comics full time, Tom expanded his artistic skills into realistic, painted pinup art. With this, he has garnered plenty of international attention and was a featured artist in the July 2006 issue of *Club International*. He was also published in *Aphrodisia 2: Art of the Female Form*.

In 2005, Tom produced two instructional DVDs with his partner Jeffrey Pederson, featuring himself and Doug Mahnke, which earned rave reviews in *Comic Buyer's Guide* and *Wizard* magazine.

Currently, Tom resides in Shakopee, MN creating full art for Marvel- and DC-related trading cards and DC Comics. He continues to work with models to produce pinups and still draws commissioned caricatures and portraits for those crazy enough to pay his ridiculously high prices. Someday Tom hopes to return to competitive bodybuilding when he isn't losing sleep over his deadlines.

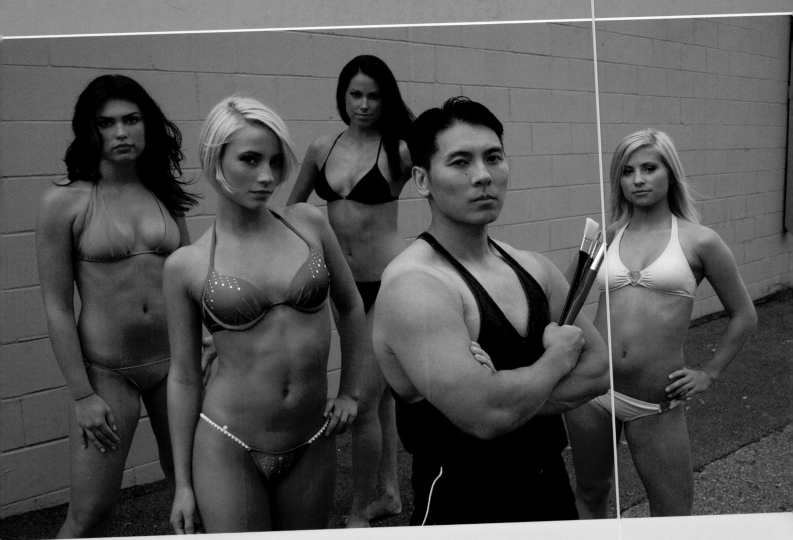

ACKNOWLEDGMENTS

I would love to thank: Pam Wissman for hunting me down and giving me this great and fun opportunity. My editors for helping me shape the vision of this book: Erin Nevius, Mona Michael, and especially Jeff Blocksidge for having the patience of a saint. Dawn Parr of Perfectly Petite, Inc. for working hard to get me exactly the look I need in my girls. My gorgeous models Hannah Gudal, Lauren Hindi, Tayeler Olson, Kristi Parrales, Aurelia Scheppers and Laura Westberg. Charlie Sackett and Robb Miller for the photos, and Romeny Chan for making us look good on the back cover! Johnny Bourlett, Adam Severin, and Iain J. Reed for their coloring assistance. Wendy Dunning for her fabulous design. Keith Champagne and David Watkins for their script contributions. Shaun Olson for helping to type what I dictated when I needed to multitask. Ken of Indigo Art for lending me his prop brushes for the photo and Peter Tomasi, for giving me my first big inking and pencilling break.

DEDICATION

To Pat Wolf, Doug Mahnke and last but not least, my parents—who came here with nothing, but gave me everything.

TABLE OF CONTENTS

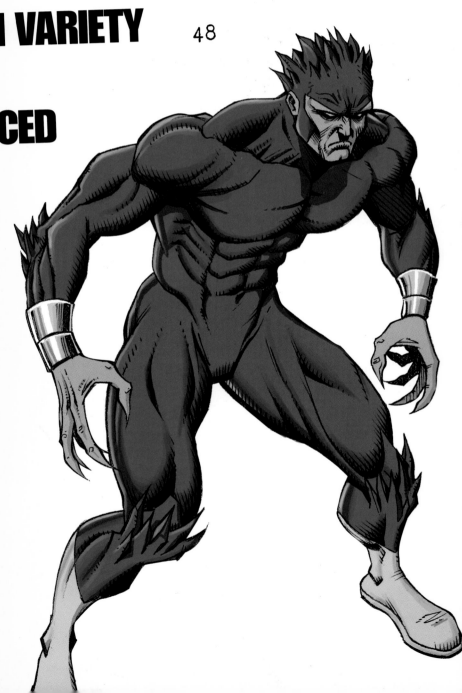

FOREWORD

I've known Tom Nguyen since his pre-professional days as a reed-thin kid with his mind affixed on being a comic pro. I still have his "self-published" WARBREED comic among the Imagesque comics I deem worthy to keep, which he wrote, pencilled, inked and edited back in his high school days. He showed all the qualities one would expect out of a kid who would make an early start in the competitive world of comics.

Years have passed since the call I received from Tom, heralding his first pro gig. He let loose with a phone-melting "YES!" My ear rang for days and eventually returned to normal, but Tom did not. Once turning pro, he has never looked back; putting in long hours and pursuing his craft with razor-sharp attention to detail. He has branched out in a variety of directions (caricature, inking, pencilling, painting, comics, cartoons, fantasy, cheesecake and portrai-

ture) and has, at the same time, built his physique into something right out of a comic book, making the average pro feel completely emasculated in his presence.

He hasn't rested for a moment, and this book is a great testament to his humor, skill, and knowledge. Tom lays it all on the table in this book ... enjoy!

Doug Mahnke, Artist, DC Comics

PS-Oh, yeah ... don't forget to check out my pencilling DVD at TomNguyenArt.com!

Backward

Tom Nguyen is an artist I envy in many ways. First, he's so short he can get into movies for the twelve-and-under price. Second, his pectoral muscles are bigger than mine. Third, he has somehow conned a large number of hot female models to pose, with little or no clothes on for him, so he can make his "art." And I guess he can draw ... a little.

Tom CLAIMS that his first art job was doing caricatures for me at a theme park in Minnesota. He actually started out as a FACE PAINTER. You know, where you paint pretty flowers on the cheeks of smelly, snot-nosed kids who are bawling because mommy wouldn't buy them their third giant stick of cotton candy. He doesn't want you to know that because most of the people I hired to do face painting were girls who had very little art skill. He thinks his shadowy past as a face painter might damage his buff, bodybuilder, macho, manly reputation. I think said reputation, or lack thereof, is safe. He can always claim that I fired him because he refused to paint designs on anyone but attractive females 18 to 25, and only then if it was anywhere but the face. In reality I fired him because his daisy designs looked suspiciously like grim reaper

heads, causing several small girls to cry uncontrollably after seeing themselves in the bathroom mirror.

Tom switched to caricatures where he could apply his talents and natural tendencies much better. Fat women stood in line for hours to receive one of his patented playmate bodies. Mysteriously he set several records for tips. Eventually, bored of theme park caricatures, he moved to comic books. The rest is history, I guess.

Tom has added a lot to his portfolio over the years. He even got paid for some. Pencils, paintings, inks, making coffee for real artists ... you name it, Tom has done it in the comics field. Now he's writing books. Despite all that, Tom is still best known for his sexy drawings of the female figure. Somehow he managed to switch from drawing fat, sweaty theme-parkers to hot, naked models. Yep, that Tom Nguyen is a guy to envy ... wish I had his pecs.

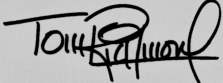

Tom Richmond, MAD Magazine

WHAT YOU NEED

Certain drawing tools and materials will aid the comic book artist greatly and are considered the standard. But remember, creativity and technical know-how (and don't forget fine motor control!) make these tools work in the first place. In any case, the following will help you get started.

PAPER

Comic book artists usually work on paper called bristol board, which is thicker than typing paper and takes pencil lead, ink, and erasing quite well. The standard size for original comic book art is 11" × 17" (28cm × 43cm). This is the size of the entire paper. The panels within the comic book page will generally fit inside a 10" × 15" (25cm × 38cm) enclosure on the board. Bristol board can be purchased in pads at your favorite art store.

This is my beautiful assistant, Tay. She'll be helping me show you the ropes throughout the book!

PENCILS

A wide variety of pencils are available to the comic book artist. Some are harder and less apt to smudge, others contain softer lead for darker lines. Soft lead smudges more easily. Pencils also come in a variety of thicknesses. Pencils need not be very sophisticated and can be as simple as a no. 2. Decide which type of pencil suits you best.

PENS AND BRUSHES

Finished comic book art is fully inked for a cleaner look and reproductive clarity. Inking your pencilled work also makes it permanent. During this stage, artists use a variety of pens and brushes with permanent black ink (India ink). Technical pens are used for ruling straight lines, curved lines, circles and ellipses. Crow quill pens which are dipped into ink and have a flexible tip are used to create a variety of widths in the inking stage. Artists may even use round-tipped brushes to help with the finer lines. These are made of quality sable hairs. Brushes come in a wide variety of shapes and sizes, of course.

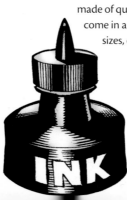

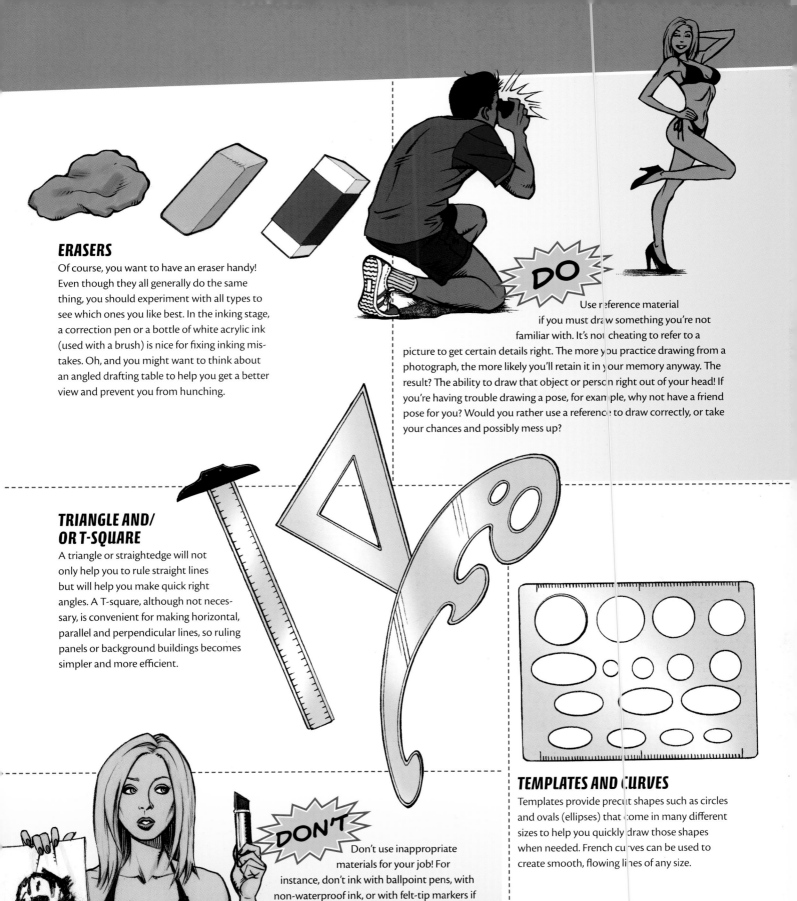

ERASERS

Of course, you want to have an eraser handy! Even though they all generally do the same thing, you should experiment with all types to see which ones you like best. In the inking stage, a correction pen or a bottle of white acrylic ink (used with a brush) is nice for fixing inking mistakes. Oh, and you might want to think about an angled drafting table to help you get a better view and prevent you from hunching.

DO

Use reference material if you must draw something you're not familiar with. It's not cheating to refer to a picture to get certain details right. The more you practice drawing from a photograph, the more likely you'll retain it in your memory anyway. The result? The ability to draw that object or person right out of your head! If you're having trouble drawing a pose, for example, why not have a friend pose for you? Would you rather use a reference to draw correctly, or take your chances and possibly mess up?

TRIANGLE AND/ OR T-SQUARE

A triangle or straightedge will not only help you to rule straight lines but will help you make quick right angles. A T-square, although not necessary, is convenient for making horizontal, parallel and perpendicular lines, so ruling panels or background buildings becomes simpler and more efficient.

DON'T

Don't use inappropriate materials for your job! For instance, don't ink with ballpoint pens, with non-waterproof ink, or with felt-tip markers if you can avoid it. Doing so may result in sloppiness, fading or bleeding. Drawing on bristol board will ensure your artwork's longevity. If you can, avoid copier paper.

TEMPLATES AND CURVES

Templates provide precut shapes such as circles and ovals (ellipses) that come in many different sizes to help you quickly draw those shapes when needed. French curves can be used to create smooth, flowing lines of any size.

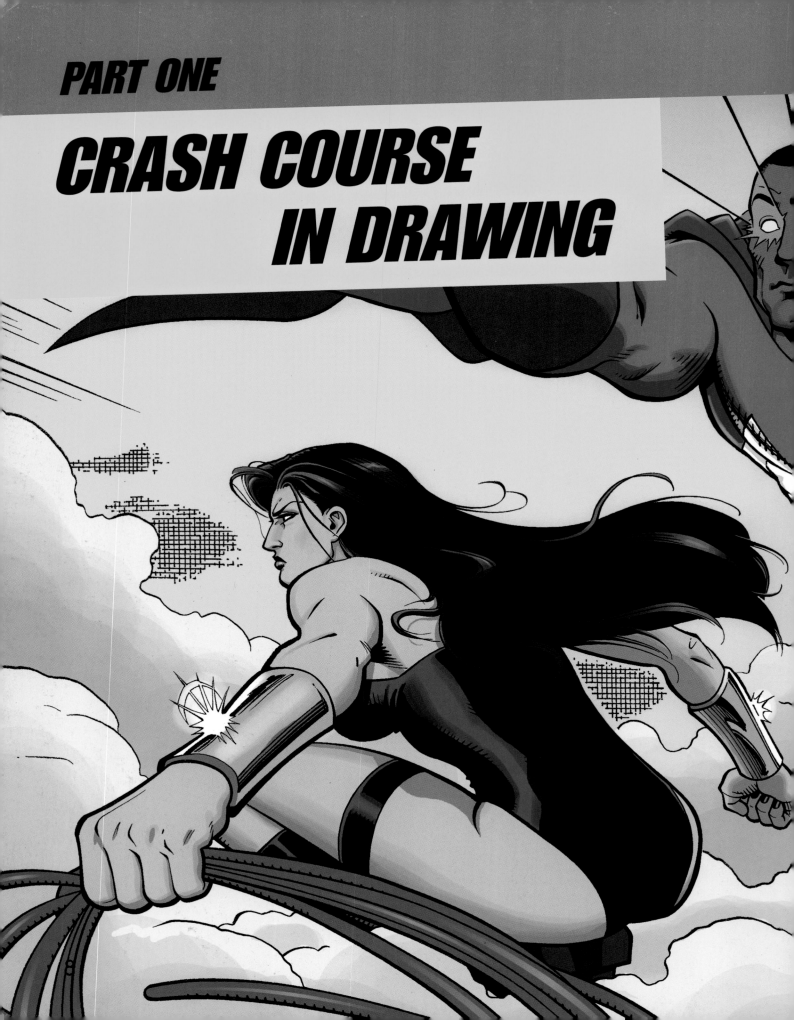

PART ONE

CRASH COURSE IN DRAWING

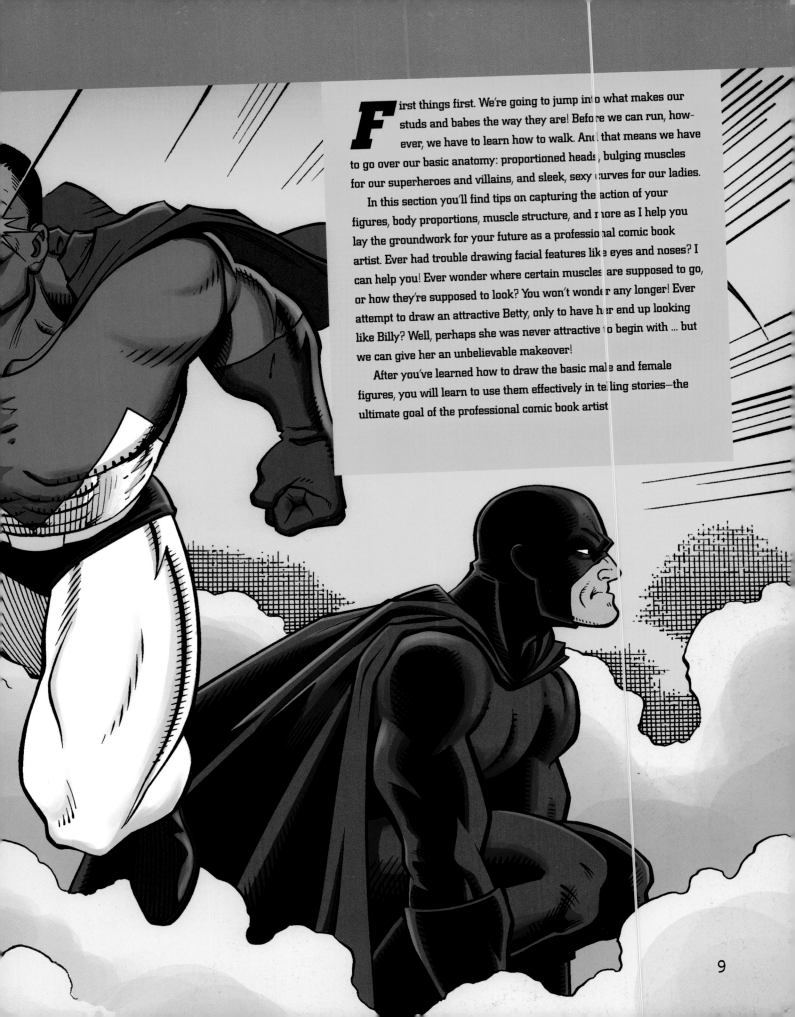

First things first. We're going to jump into what makes our studs and babes the way they are! Before we can run, however, we have to learn how to walk. And that means we have to go over our basic anatomy: proportioned heads, bulging muscles for our superheroes and villains, and sleek, sexy curves for our ladies.

In this section you'll find tips on capturing the action of your figures, body proportions, muscle structure, and more as I help you lay the groundwork for your future as a professional comic book artist. Ever had trouble drawing facial features like eyes and noses? I can help you! Ever wonder where certain muscles are supposed to go, or how they're supposed to look? You won't wonder any longer! Ever attempt to draw an attractive Betty, only to have her end up looking like Billy? Well, perhaps she was never attractive to begin with ... but we can give her an unbelievable makeover!

After you've learned how to draw the basic male and female figures, you will learn to use them effectively in telling stories—the ultimate goal of the professional comic book artist.

GESTURE DRAWING *& Rough Sketching*

Where to begin? When drawing a figure, the answer is a gesture sketch. But even then, should one begin with the head? The eyes? The toes!? Start broadly with the centerline and capture the figure's essence.

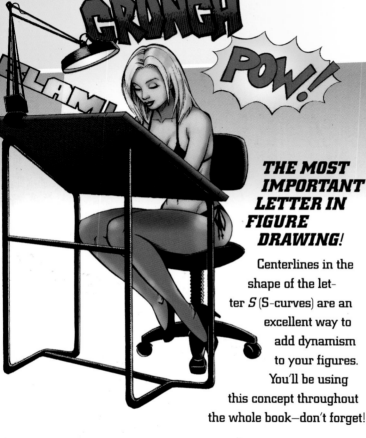

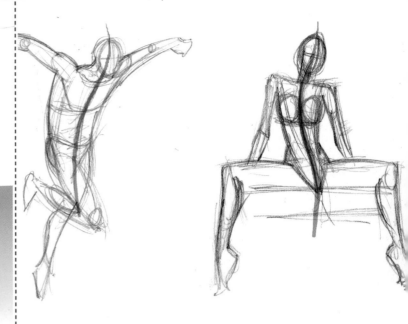

THE MOST IMPORTANT LETTER IN FIGURE DRAWING!

Centerlines in the shape of the letter *S* (S-curves) are an excellent way to add dynamism to your figures. You'll be using this concept throughout the whole book—don't forget!

DEMONSTRATION

HOW TO BEGIN A GESTURE DRAWING

Begin with a centerline to establish the posture of the body. After roughing in general movements and proportional divisions, we can work smaller with more jazz and detail.

Yawn, right? Knock this beginning stuff out first and everything onward will be easier and more fun, I promise!

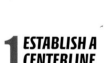

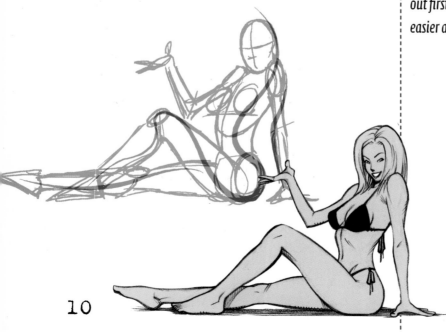

1 ESTABLISH A CENTERLINE

Generally, the more straight up and down the line is, the stiffer the figure will be. The more diagonal, the more dynamic and fluid your figure.

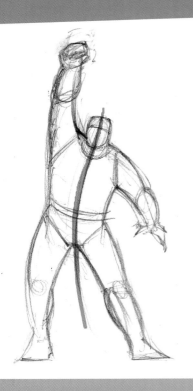

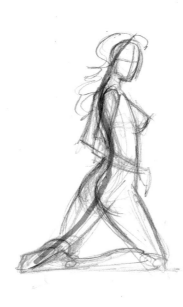

THE CENTERLINE

See how within the gesture drawings, you can make out a centerline that runs through the entire figure? This centerline (also called the line of action) is often the first line that is put down to immediately establish the direction of the figure's movement and the posture of the body.

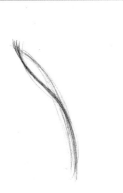 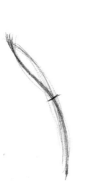 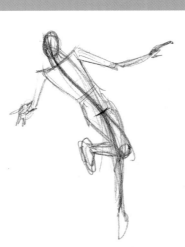

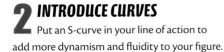

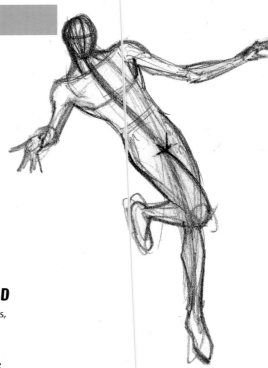

2 INTRODUCE CURVES

Put an S-curve in your line of action to add more dynamism and fluidity to your figure.

3 ESTABLISH THE CENTER POINT

The center point will be the crotch area where the legs will branch out. The upper half of the line will be the upper body. You may raise this division line a tad above center for females because they are often portrayed with longer legs—but no need to sweat the details.

4 ADD THE ARMS, LEGS AND HEAD

Establish the motion of the arms and legs, then attach the head. Keep everything fluid, fast and sketchy to maintain kinetic energy. All you're trying to do is establish action in the most intriguing way.

5 ROUND OUT AND FINISH

Although not necessary for rough sketching, you can now add more shaping and detail to begin the real drawing.

PRACTICE GESTURE DRAWINGS

MEN

These are examples of male figures sketched in gesture. Again, notice how the centerline is the basis of the direction and action of the figure. The overall gesture sketches are just that: sketchy. Stay loose and fast! You just want to capture the essence of the action (or inaction) in this stage.

OUR MAN IN GESTURE

Though not clean or accurate, the point of gesture drawings is to get the ideas, expression and motion down quickly. Doing it this way preserves the dynamic energy and movement in your art and figures. If you fail to get this energy down, your resulting figures will look stiff and unexciting.

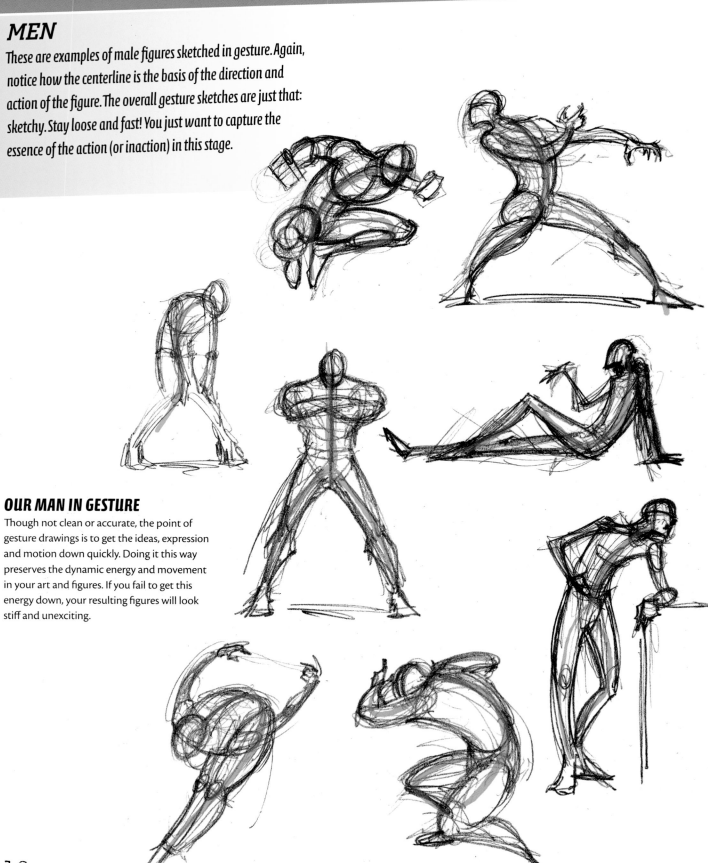

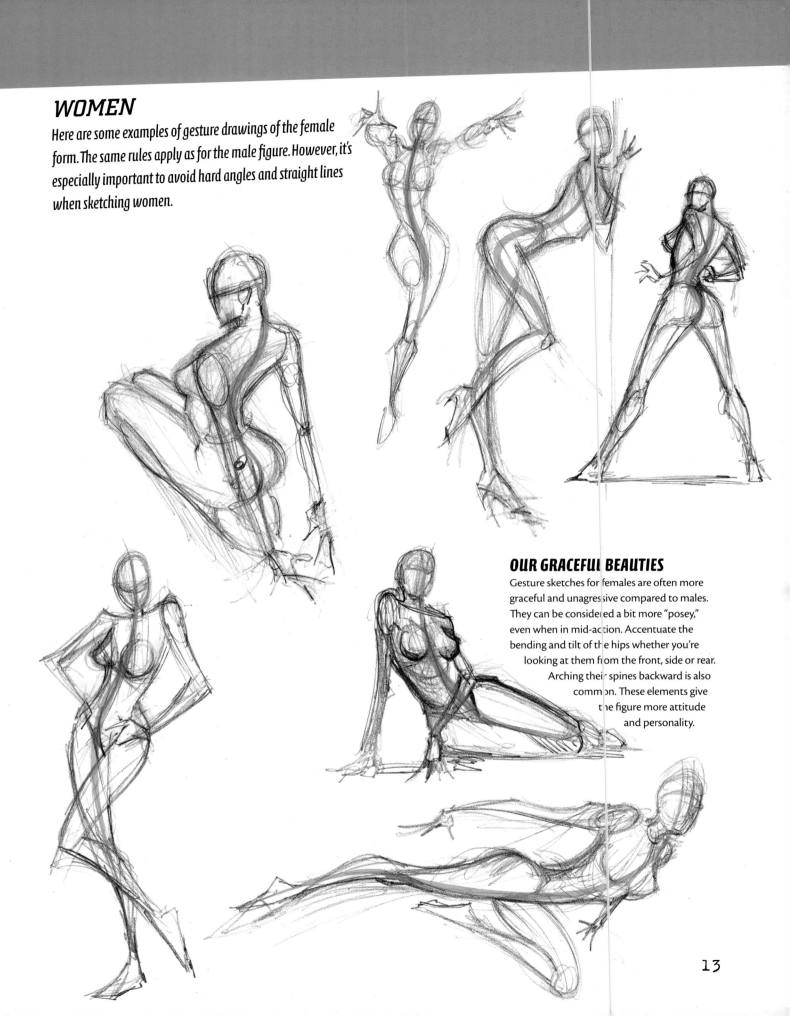

WOMEN

Here are some examples of gesture drawings of the female form. The same rules apply as for the male figure. However, it's especially important to avoid hard angles and straight lines when sketching women.

OUR GRACEFUL BEAUTIES

Gesture sketches for females are often more graceful and unaggressive compared to males. They can be considered a bit more "posey," even when in mid-action. Accentuate the bending and tilt of the hips whether you're looking at them from the front, side or rear. Arching their spines backward is also common. These elements give the figure more attitude and personality.

13

DRAWING STUD MUFFINS & REAL BAD DUDES

Let's start off with learning the general proportions of your typical, handsome, muscular male hero, a.k.a. the stud muffin. We'll take a simple approach and go over special tips to keep in mind as you practice drawing your overall male figure. We'll review individual body parts in detail later. For now, we have the basic front, back and side views of our handsome guy.

THE FRONT VIEW

Since it is easiest to measure from the center, you should note that the center of the length of the body (from head to toe) is the crotch. The length of the body above the crotch can be mentally divided into fourths. The very top fourth is the head itself. The second fourth, which is one head-length down, will end around the nipple area. The third fourth, which is about one head length up from the crotch, is where the bellybutton will be.

The lower half of the entire body (from the crotch down) is composed of the legs and feet. About halfway down the legs is where you would naturally find the knees.

THE BACK VIEW

The silhouettes of both the front and back views are identical; only when lighted would you see the different arrangement of the muscle groups. Keep in mind where the contours cut in front of each other here because it would be the opposite of how they are portrayed in the front view.

THE SIDE VIEW

Notice that not all of the body parts are perfectly aligned in a straight up-and-down manner. Once again, it's important to notice the S-shaped patterns that are repeated when looking at the figure from this angle.

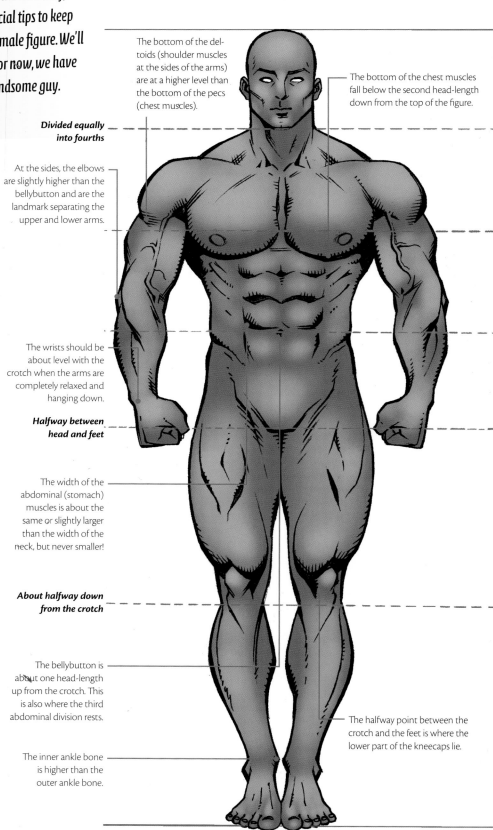

The bottom of the deltoids (shoulder muscles at the sides of the arms) are at a higher level than the bottom of the pecs (chest muscles).

The bottom of the chest muscles fall below the second head-length down from the top of the figure.

Divided equally into fourths

At the sides, the elbows are slightly higher than the bellybutton and are the landmark separating the upper and lower arms.

The wrists should be about level with the crotch when the arms are completely relaxed and hanging down.

Halfway between head and feet

The width of the abdominal (stomach) muscles is about the same or slightly larger than the width of the neck, but never smaller!

About halfway down from the crotch

The bellybutton is about one head-length up from the crotch. This is also where the third abdominal division rests.

The inner ankle bone is higher than the outer ankle bone.

The halfway point between the crotch and the feet is where the lower part of the kneecaps lie.

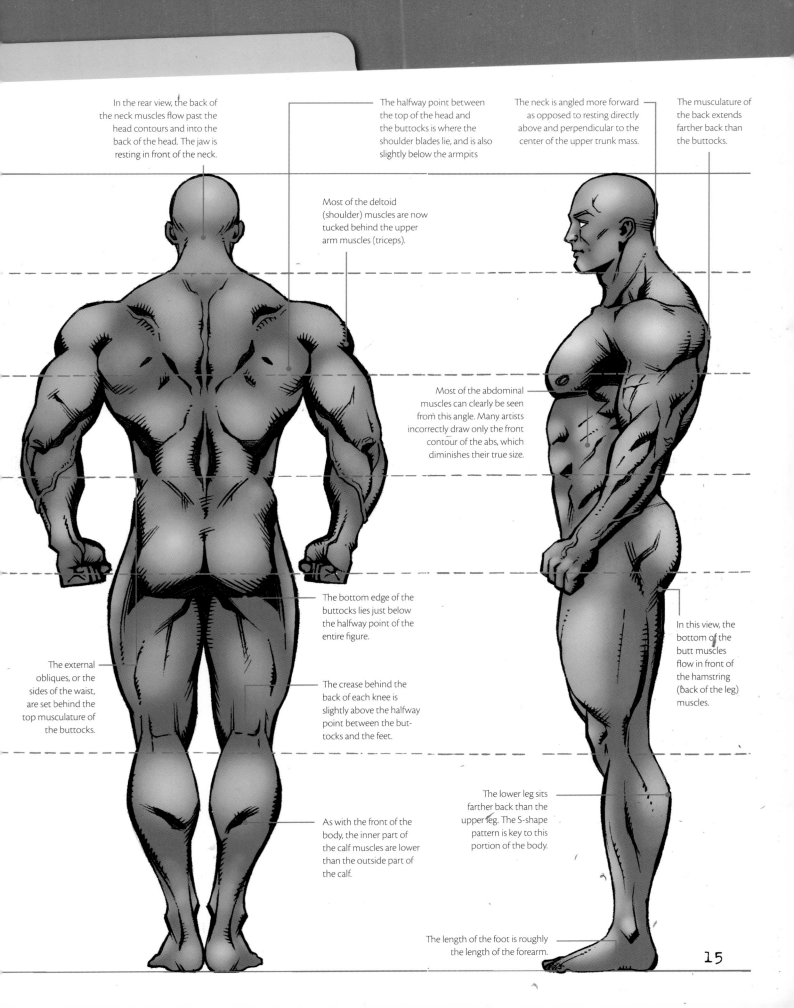

In the rear view, the back of the neck muscles flow past the head contours and into the back of the head. The jaw is resting in front of the neck.

The halfway point between the top of the head and the buttocks is where the shoulder blades lie, and is also slightly below the armpits

The neck is angled more forward as opposed to resting directly above and perpendicular to the center of the upper trunk mass.

The musculature of the back extends farther back than the buttocks.

Most of the deltoid (shoulder) muscles are now tucked behind the upper arm muscles (triceps).

Most of the abdominal muscles can clearly be seen from this angle. Many artists incorrectly draw only the front contour of the abs, which diminishes their true size.

The bottom edge of the buttocks lies just below the halfway point of the entire figure.

The external obliques, or the sides of the waist, are set behind the top musculature of the buttocks.

The crease behind the back of each knee is slightly above the halfway point between the buttocks and the feet.

In this view, the bottom of the butt muscles flow in front of the hamstring (back of the leg) muscles.

The lower leg sits farther back than the upper leg. The S-shape pattern is key to this portion of the body.

As with the front of the body, the inner part of the calf muscles are lower than the outside part of the calf.

The length of the foot is roughly the length of the forearm.

15

THE HANDSOME HERO'S HEAD AND FACE

Let's face it (pun intended!), the head and face are what we notice first on a person. Here are some simple guidelines to help you draw them more confidently. These are especially useful when you don't have references handy. Who needs them anyway?

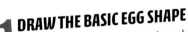

FRONT VIEW

Looking straight on, the head looks roughly egg-shaped with the rounder emphasis on the top half. A horizontal line through the middle of the "egg" will divide it into upper and lower halves, and will serve as the guideline for where the eyes should be placed. About halfway between the eye line and the bottom of the chin is where the bottom of the nose should be. The mouth should be anywhere between one-third to one-half of the way down from the bottom of the nose (usually just a tad above halfway between the nose and chin). The ears fit snugly between the eye level and nose level. The width of the head is generally five eyes wide, with one eye's width between the eyes and on either side. The corners of the mouth generally line up under the center of each eye.

1 DRAW THE BASIC EGG SHAPE
Start with a basic egg shape and rough in your vertical and horizontal guidelines.

2 PLACE GUIDELINES AND ROUGH FEATURES
Put in additional guidelines and begin roughing in the placement of your features.

3 RENDER, MODIFY AND FINISH
Finish off with tight rendering, modifying any facial features to your desire. Your drawing will be well-constructed because you've sketched in your basic shape and guidelines.

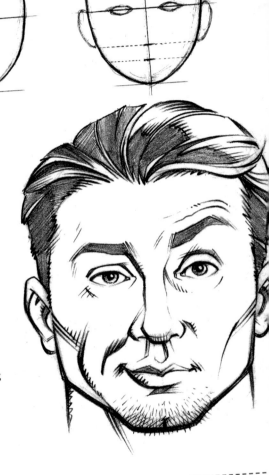

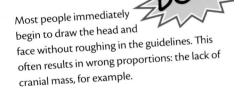

NO COVER-UPS!

Avoid adding excessive lines and crosshatching in an attempt to add more detail or cover up your lack of basic structure. You'll improve faster.

Most people immediately begin to draw the head and face without roughing in the guidelines. This often results in wrong proportions: the lack of cranial mass, for example.

DON'T

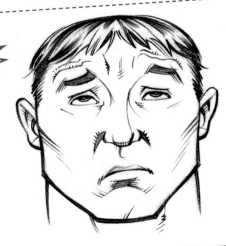

SIDE VIEW

The side of the head is basically a round circle for the cranium, and then a triangular wedge hanging off one side for the face. A horizontal line at the halfway-point between the top and bottom gives us the eye line again—just like the front. Next, look at the top of the circle you've sketched. If you draw a vertical line straight down the middle of the circle from this top, you will see that the ear will fall slightly behind this line.

In other ways the profile of the head is the same as the front: the bottom of the nose would end about halfway between the eye line and the bottom of the chin, and the ears fall between the eyes and the nose.

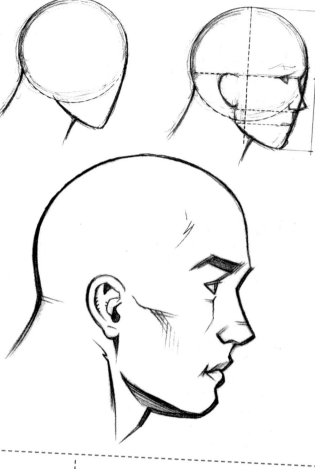

1 SKETCH YOUR CIRCLE AND WEDGE
Begin by sketching in a circle, then add a triangular wedge hanging off one side. This wedge will be the lower half of the face in profile.

2 DRAW GUIDELINES FOR FEATURES
The ears, as in the front view, fall between the eye line and nose line. A horizontal line from the mouth will run right into the corner of the jaw.

3 FINISH
Finish off your drawing and be confident that it will look right!

THREE-QUARTER VIEW

Pay attention to the vertical line that runs through the center of the nose. The farther the head is turned, the farther this line moves away from the centerline. Keep track of the space between them—it's the same amount you add to the back of the cranium as more of it shows.

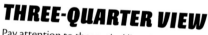

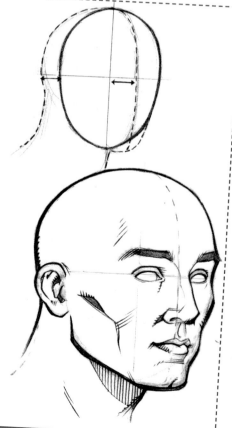

1 START WITH THE FRONT
Divide the face as you would for the front and side views and use the guidelines to rough in your features. Pay attention to the centerline, it will guide us as to how far the head is turned.

2 FINISH
Finish the drawing using the guidelines. It may take some practice to get the features right but what else are you going to do today?

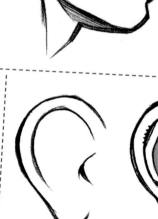

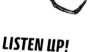

LISTEN UP!
When drawing the ear, first notice the outer rim and the *tragus* (the little knob of cartilage in front of the ear canal). Then visualize a curved Y-shape within the ear to form the rest.

EYES, LIPS AND MOUTH

Who hasn't come across a blood-curdling sneer or dagger eyes in comics? Learn the basics of facial features and later you'll be able to say so much by changing them slightly.

  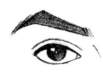

FOR THE GUYS

Men's eyebrows tend to be thicker, with different ways of feathering off. Sometimes you may want to show some eyelashes in your guys; this can be done without feminizing them! Generally, use more lines around the eyes of guys to show structure or wrinkles and folds. (You can't get away with this on women!) Notice that not only is the eyelid size varied, but so is the shape.

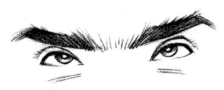

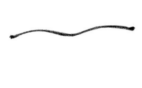

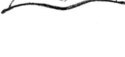

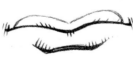

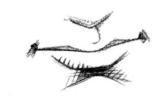 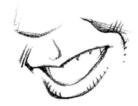

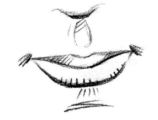 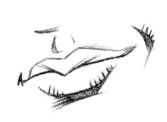

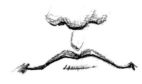

1 THE M-SHAPE
Pay close attention to the M-shape (or lack thereof in some cases) of the upper lip and how it varies in shape and length. Start in the middle and branch outwards.

2 TOP OF THE UPPER LIP
Draw the top edge of the upper lip, which may also resemble an "M."

3 THE THICKER LOWER LIP
The full, lower lip is often thicker than the upper lip. Draw it with a good undershadow.

SO MANY TO FEED, SO LITTLE TIME
Here are a variety of manly mouths. Don't forget to vary the teeth and amount of gums showing.

NOSES

Noses are fun to mess around with because they have so much potential for variety and character. Most comic book women are drawn with a cute little upturned nose; for the fellas, well, just about anything goes here! Check out the various nose bridges and bumps and nostrils that we have to choose from. There's no reason all of our characters need to look the same!

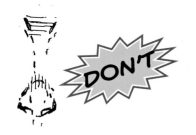

VISUALIZE THE SHAPE

The general shape of the nose is a triangular wedge. Visualize this shape rotating when you're drawing the nose. Play with its shape to introduce variety in your sniffers.

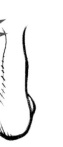
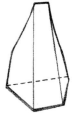

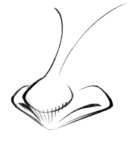
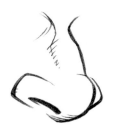
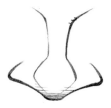

FROM SCHNOZ TO PROBOSCIS

The sky's the limit for noses on guys. They actually seem to add more character and charm to the male face. Mess around with them, but don't just play with size; have fun with the nostrils and tip too!

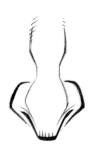
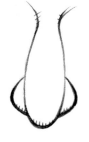
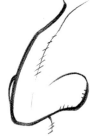
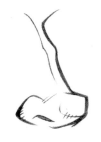
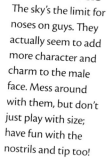

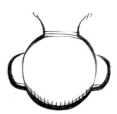
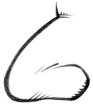
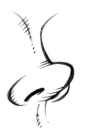

19

BICEPS

Many times muscular arms are drawn with huge biceps, and small everything else. In our culture, the biceps have become ingrained as THE muscle of the arms. It is, after all, the one flexed most often for show. But it looks quite ridiculous when drawn bigger than the deltoid (shoulder) muscles and triceps (back of the arm).

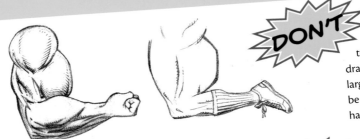

DON'T The arm functions in a way similar to the leg. To draw abnormally large biceps would be like drawing huge hamstrings.

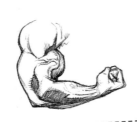
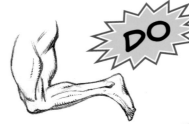

DO Keep the biceps close in size to the deltoid (shoulder) muscles.

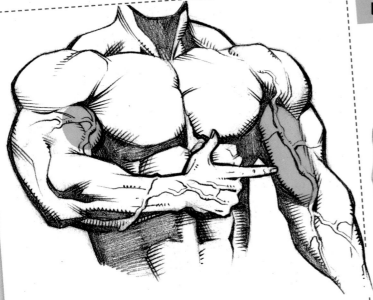

BICEPS CHANGE SHAPE
See how when the arm is straightened, the biceps tend to have a longer, straighter shape to it before it dips into the elbow. When the arm is curled up, the biceps are shortened into more of a ball shape.

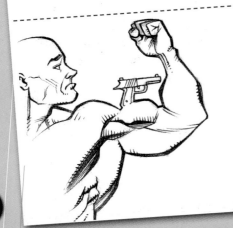

Lock and Load?
Unfortunately, the biceps in no way resemble a gun, so drawing one won't help you.

DEMONSTRATION

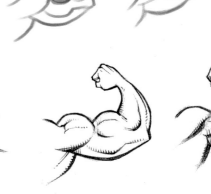

1 ROUGH OUT CORRECTLY FIRST
The bicep is often mistakenly drawn very large. Make sure the length of the deltoid is about the same as the length of the bicep. When flexing, a good rule is to keep the deltoid and bicep humps the same size. Many artists will incorrectly draw the brachialis muscle as part of the bicep.

2 FINISH TO SHOW FORM
When you finish your arm drawing, add extra darkness under each bulge of muscle with small hatching coming from it to give it dimensionality.

TRICEPS

Think about this: did you know that the triceps (back of the arm) are roughly two-thirds of your upper-arm mass? That's right, and yet it is often ignored in drawing in favor of the biceps. The triceps can be seen from every angle; the same cannot be said of the biceps.

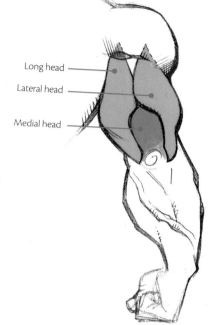

Long head
Lateral head
Medial head

THE BRACHIORADIALIS

This muscle is easier to show than explain: it's that gnarly, thick forearm muscle that starts at the side of the biceps, butts against the triceps and curls its way down.

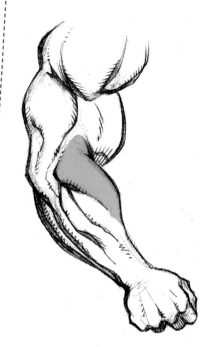

MUSCLE GRAMMAR

Notice that when you're looking at the right arm from the side, the triceps is simply shaped like a comma (reverse the "comma" for the left arm).

THE THREE-HEADED MUSCLE

The triceps—aptly named—is made of three heads: the long (inside) head, the lateral (side) head, and the medial (middle) head. The distinctive horseshoe shape and its indentation provide a great start to drawing this muscle.

THINK TBBB

Here is the simple outlining of the arm's musculature from the side. Many people are lost when it comes to the correct place-ment of these muscles. The *brachioradialis* is located between the triceps and the *brachialis* (related to the biceps, also assists in pulling). Think of the arm's muscles as TBBB: Triceps, Brachioradialis, Brachialis, and Biceps. Keep the all the Bs together, and the triceps are on either side depending on which arm you're looking at.

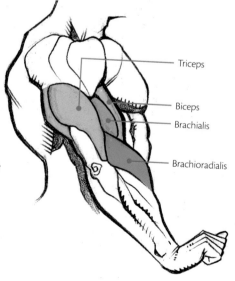

Triceps
Biceps
Brachialis
Brachioradialis

BOUNCING PECS

The pectoralis major muscles (chest muscles) are flat slabs of beef on the front of your body, and are used to pull the arms inward and across the body as if you were doing a big bear hug. As shown before on the proportions chart (pages 14–15), the nipples on the chest are approximately one head-length down from the chin. The chest muscle will curve just underneath that.

START FROM THE ARMPIT

The chest muscle's point of origin is the armpit from which it fans out toward the collarbone and sternum. Use the armpit as a reference point for where the chest, biceps and deltoid muscles meet.

DON'T

DO

MUSCLE ASSEMBLY

Notice how the chest muscle striations are drawn horizontally in the first example. The second example shows the correct way to draw chest muscles: Fan them out appropriately from the armpit's point of origin.

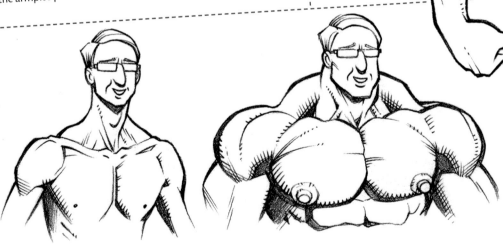

CLEAVAGE AND COLLAR BONES? OR JUST PLAIN BEEF?

Unless your male figure is extremely muscular, you will always see the sternum as a flat area of "cleavage" between each pec and the collarbone. However, if your male figure is heavily muscled, the collarbone and sternum will seem to disappear. The muscles fill in these gaps.

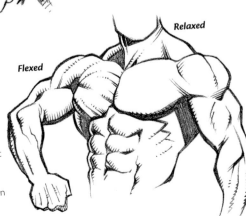

Relaxed

Flexed

Hey Girls
When the chest is flexed, you'll see more striations than when relaxed.

WASHBOARD ABS

What's a rock-hard body without a set of six-pack abdominal muscles? Always the showcase muscle, it seems absolutely necessary in order to complete the package of a superhero stud. Although muscular abs are generally drawn with at least a faint indication of separation, their pronunciation is greatly increased as they do their function of crunching the body. We'll touch upon the surrounding muscles, too.

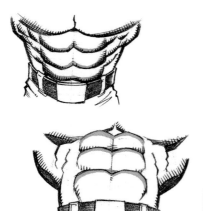

W AND M

Looking down, notice and utilize a pattern of Ws in the abs' shape. Looking up, draw abs at an upward angle using M-shapes.

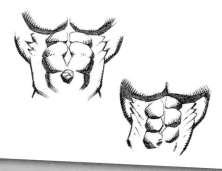

DEMONSTRATION

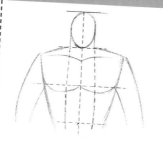

1 SIZE UP YOUR SIX-PACK
You want your abs at least as wide as your neck—perhaps even a little wider.

2 DIVIDE SPACE AND ROUGH IN
Remember, in your average superhero the space between the nipples and the bellybutton is about one head-length. Divide that space into thirds and you have the six-pack blueprint.

3 TIGHTEN AND SQUEEZE!
Tighten up your drawing. It should be a cinch if you've got your proportions correct. Carefully position your light source when rendering the abs. Keep the light and shadows consistent with the rest of the body.

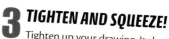

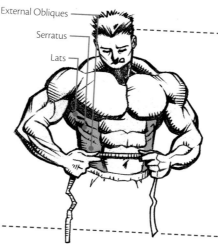

External Obliques

Serratus

Lats

VISUALIZE MUSCLE COLUMNS
Moving outward on either side, we have the *external obliques*, the *serratus* muscles, and the *latissimus dorsi* ("widest back" in Latin) or lats of the back. If you think of the abs as two vertical columns (each containing three segments), make sure that each external oblique column is a little thinner than an abdominal column.

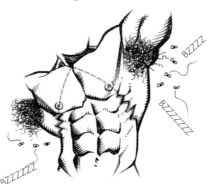

FIND THE OBLIQUE-SERRATUS BORDER
Many people have trouble placing where the obliques intertwine with the serratus muscles. If you imagine a line from the pit of the neck (where the collarbones meet) across the chest and past the nipple, this is where you would define the "shark's teeth" of the oblique-serratus border. This jagged shape is all you really need.

COBRA HOOD BACKS

Why are backs so hard to draw? In comics, you don't draw talking scenes with the characters' backs to the viewer all the time. This lack of attention to the back causes it to be misdrawn so often in comics. Here are tips to help you understand and draw the back muscles more effectively.

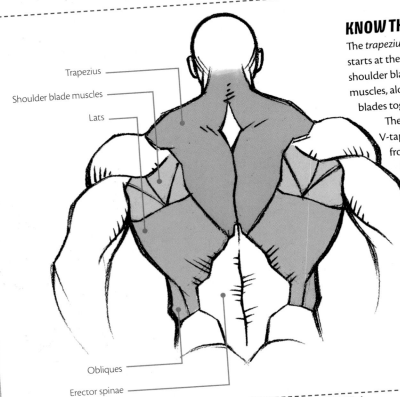

Trapezius
Shoulder blade muscles
Lats
Obliques
Erector spinae

KNOW THE MUSCLES OF THE BACK

The *trapezius* (or simply "traps") muscle is roughly diamond shaped. It starts at the base of the neck, connects to the upper protrusion of the shoulder blades, and bottoms out around the middle of the back. These muscles, along with the lats, are responsible for pulling your shoulder blades together—for instance, if you were to pull towards you.

The lats are the big side muscles of the back that help define the V-taper of the upper body. Most people naturally draw that taper from the armpits to the waist anyway, so that's a start. To keep it simple, start near the armpits and flow down in front of the external obliques (see the abs section on page 23). Each lat forms a V at the bottom and goes back up to meet the bottom of the traps.

Learn the basic shapes and placement of the minor muscles in relation to the major back muscles to draw some serious mass.

DIAL M

Another way to view the traps is to see the M-shape that it forms with the vertical protrusion of the shoulder blades.

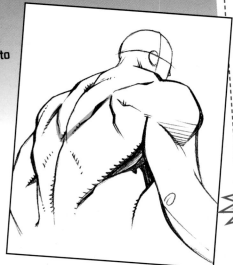

DON'T

This guy fell victim to a horridly drawn back. The only things remotely correct are the centerline for the spine and the cobra-hood-like lats. Knowing how to connect those muscles can be tricky if you're not familiar with any of the other supporting back muscles.

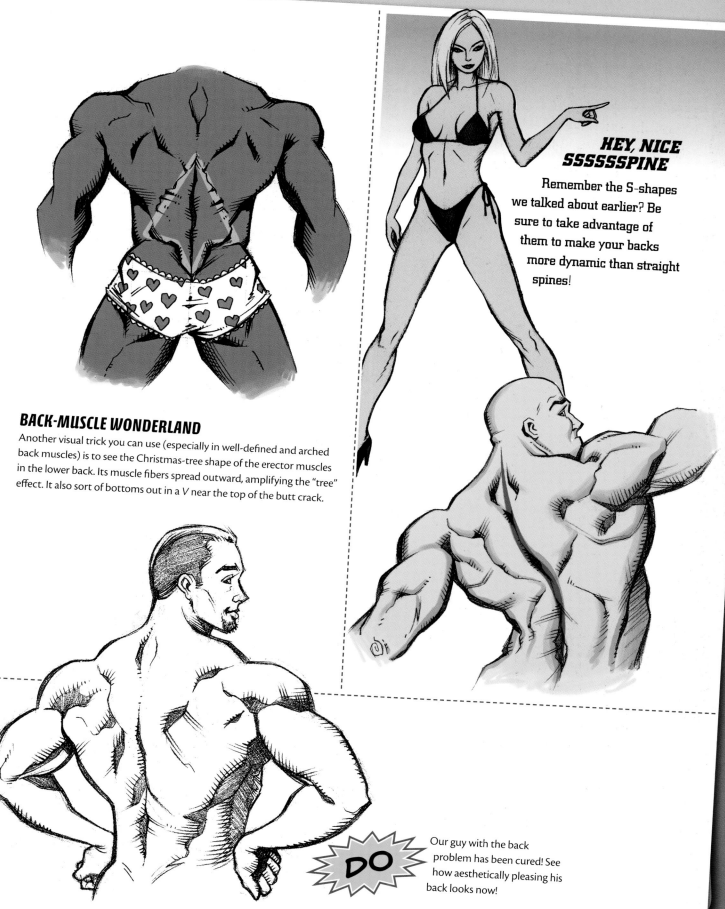

Remember the S-shapes we talked about earlier? Be sure to take advantage of them to make your backs more dynamic than straight spines!

BACK-MUSCLE WONDERLAND

Another visual trick you can use (especially in well-defined and arched back muscles) is to see the Christmas-tree shape of the erector muscles in the lower back. Its muscle fibers spread outward, amplifying the "tree" effect. It also sort of bottoms out in a *V* near the top of the butt crack.

DO

Our guy with the back problem has been cured! See how aesthetically pleasing his back looks now!

25

BRUTAL LEGS

With such muscular upper bodies, we need equally massive legs to support them. How silly would it look to have huge arms, shoulders and chests resting on a pair of toothpicks? Aspiring artists often focus on drawing the upper body so much, they ignore the lower body. This results in poor, awkwardly drawn legs. Here are some tips to help turn those twigs into oak trees!

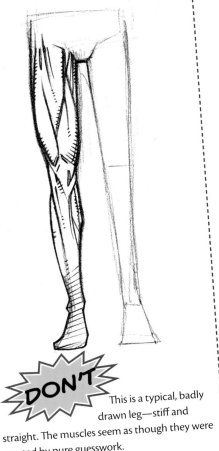

DON'T This is a typical, badly drawn leg—stiff and straight. The muscles seem as though they were created by pure guesswork.

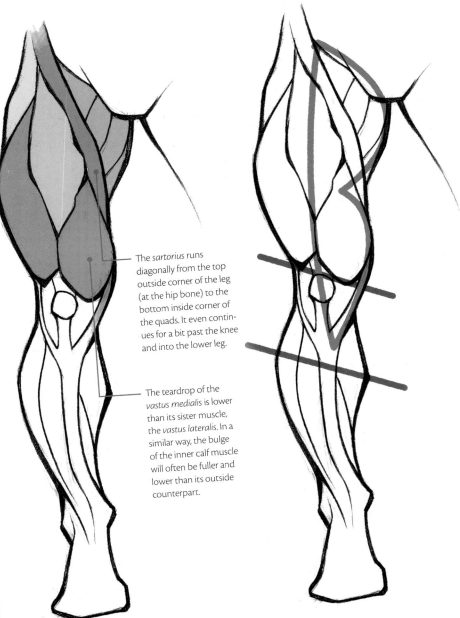

The *sartorius* runs diagonally from the top outside corner of the leg (at the hip bone) to the bottom inside corner of the quads. It even continues for a bit past the knee and into the lower leg.

The teardrop of the *vastus medialis* is lower than its sister muscle, the *vastus lateralis*. In a similar way, the bulge of the inner calf muscle will often be fuller and lower than its outside counterpart.

KNOW THE MUSCLES OF THE LEG

The legs start very thickly at the top, then gradually narrow as they taper toward the knees. The muscle group on the front of the thigh makes up the *quadriceps*. These muscles begin at the hip and join at the knee. Together, they straighten out the leg from a bent-knee position. The quads are so named because they are comprised of four muscles, though only three are visible.

A good visual feature to remember is the prominent, teardrop shape of the *vastus medialis*. Also, the contour of the inner thighs tend to take on a B-shape (reverse the B for the left leg).

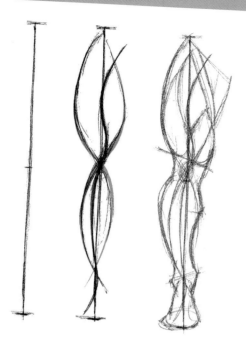

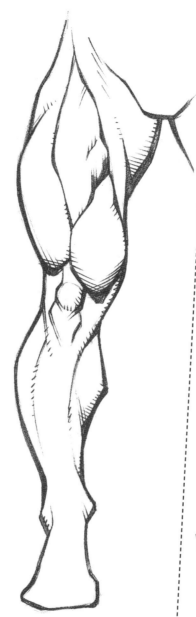

1 ESTABLISH THE LENGTH

Remember that the length of the legs is about equal to the length of the upper body from the top of the head to the crotch. In other words, the legs make up the entire lower half of the body. Establish their length first. Then mark halfway down; the knee will be immediately above this mark.

2 OUTLINE THE SHAPE

The legs should never be drawn in a straight line, no matter the angle! Use the ever-trusty S-shape. This will make your legs look lively and natural.

3 ROUGH IN THE MUSCLES

Rough in the muscle outlines, incorporating the tips from these diagrams.

4 FINISH!

Finish off with clean, tight lines.

FOLLOW THE CURVES

Curves and S-shapes are always used in legs—always! These initial shapes are the foundation of successful, dynamic legs. If you're having trouble drawing different angles or foreshortening your legs, try sketching the gridlike cylindrical shapes of the upper and lower leg.

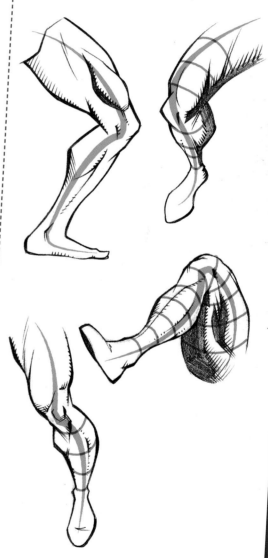

KNOWING WHEN TO STOP

As with faces, it's important to know when to stop when it comes to rendering male figures. Besides the fact that many extra, unnecessary lines are often used to cover up mistakes, more lines may simulate texture rather than form. This will flatten the drawing, preventing you from maximizing the lights and darks to convey dimensionality.

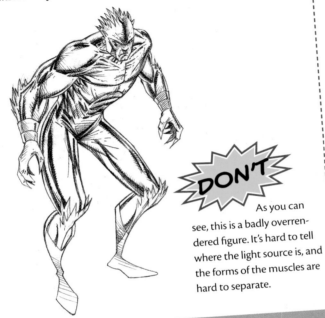

DON'T

As you can see, this is a badly overrendered figure. It's hard to tell where the light source is, and the forms of the muscles are hard to separate.

OH, NO! I'M FORESHORTENED!

Foreshortening is a form of perspective where a basic object's shape is tilted and skewed—usually towards the viewer—where one side of it is closer than the other. If drawn effectively, your mind's eye will "fill in the details" and will recognize it as being the same object, just at a different angle within the same space.

When doing any type of foreshortening, hatching in the direction of your object's contours is a great way to effectively render it!

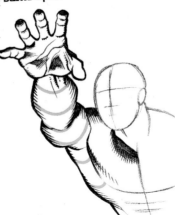

Light source

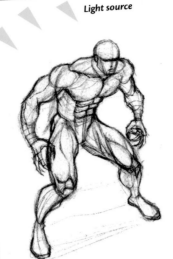

1 ESTABLISH THE BASICS

Rough out your drawing. Establish the basic proportions and where you want everything placed. Pick a light source. The simplest source of light is above and slightly to the side.

2 DEFINE THE MUSCLES

Begin defining the side of each muscle group (or any other individual form) away from the light (in shadow). In this case, the lines defined are the bottom and bottom-right of each muscle and form.

HARSH LIGHTS = HARSH SHADOWS

If your light source is intense and concentrated (i.e., a spotlight overhead), add black alongside the edges that are away from this light. Then you may add very short feathering from these black lines if you choose to. Using long feathering will defeat the purpose of intense lighting.

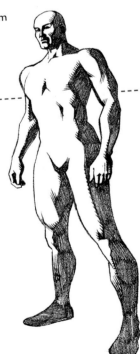

DRAWING STUD MUFFINS & REAL BAD DUDES

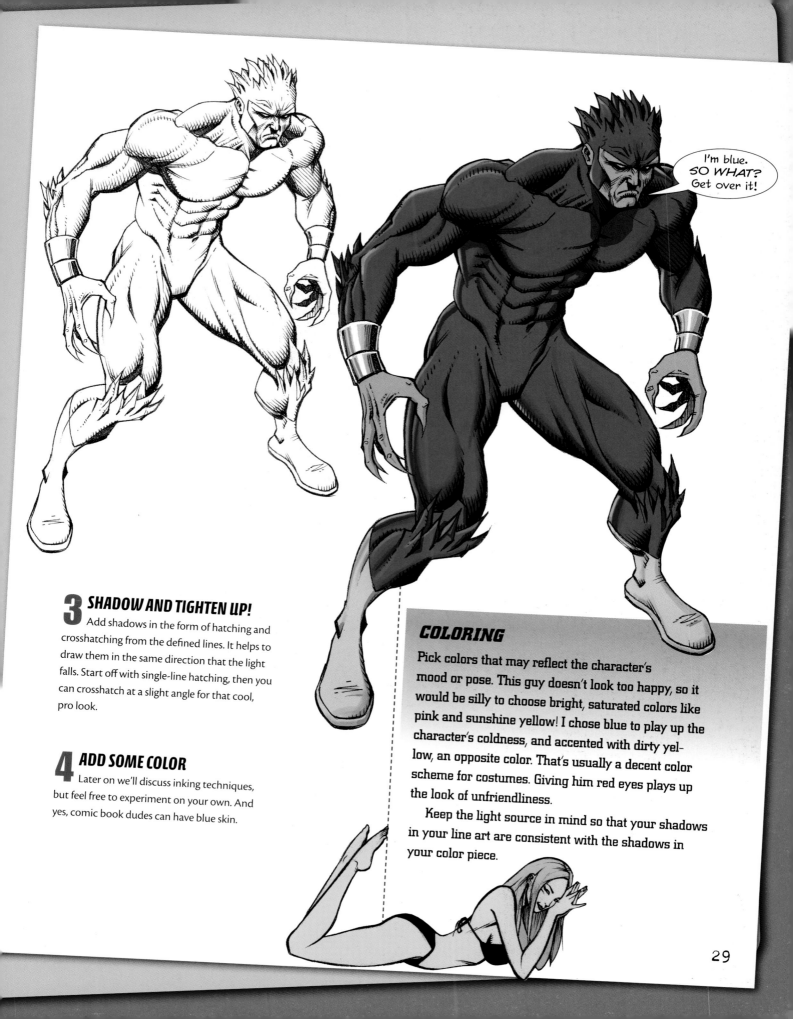

I'm blue. SO *WHAT?* Get over it!

3 SHADOW AND TIGHTEN UP!

Add shadows in the form of hatching and crosshatching from the defined lines. It helps to draw them in the same direction that the light falls. Start off with single-line hatching, then you can crosshatch at a slight angle for that cool, pro look.

4 ADD SOME COLOR

Later on we'll discuss inking techniques, but feel free to experiment on your own. And yes, comic book dudes can have blue skin.

COLORING

Pick colors that may reflect the character's mood or pose. This guy doesn't look too happy, so it would be silly to choose bright, saturated colors like pink and sunshine yellow! I chose blue to play up the character's coldness, and accented with dirty yellow, an opposite color. That's usually a decent color scheme for costumes. Giving him red eyes plays up the look of unfriendliness.

Keep the light source in mind so that your shadows in your line art are consistent with the shadows in your color piece.

29

RELAX!

When you are drawing muscular superheroes, it can be very tempting to draw every last little muscle and striation in order to make your character look as buff as possible. Heck, you may even stack made-up muscles on the ones you've already drawn! But it's very important to know when to lay off the graphite in situations where the character is in a relaxed state—his head might explode from tensing and straining all day! Many scenes in comic art call for this, and a good artist should know when and how to use poses that show less flexing. So how do we show that a superhero is both buff and relaxed at the same time? Check out these examples for tips.

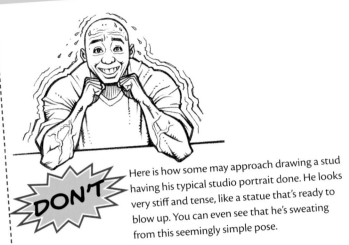

DON'T

Here is how some may approach drawing a stud having his typical studio portrait done. He looks very stiff and tense, like a statue that's ready to blow up. You can even see that he's sweating from this seemingly simple pose.

DEMONSTRATION

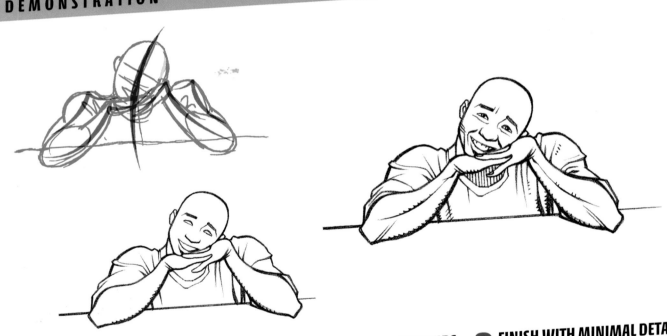

1 ROUGH IN WITH CURVES
When you begin to rough in your gesture drawing (remember that from page 10?), use a lot of sweeping curves. Use S-curves where appropriate. This eliminates rigidity in your poses. Use quick, light strokes. If your angle is a straight-on shot such as this one, use some asymmetry to tilt things a bit. This helps maintain a looser, more animated pose.

2 DEFINE FORM WITH CONTOURS
Draw the contours to define the form. Try to maintain the animated looseness you had in your gesture drawing by keeping some of the sweeping curves.

3 FINISH WITH MINIMAL DETAIL
Finish by drawing just the key muscle bulges, with minimal feathering to show a little more form. Avoid drawing any unnecessary muscles, striations or hatching.

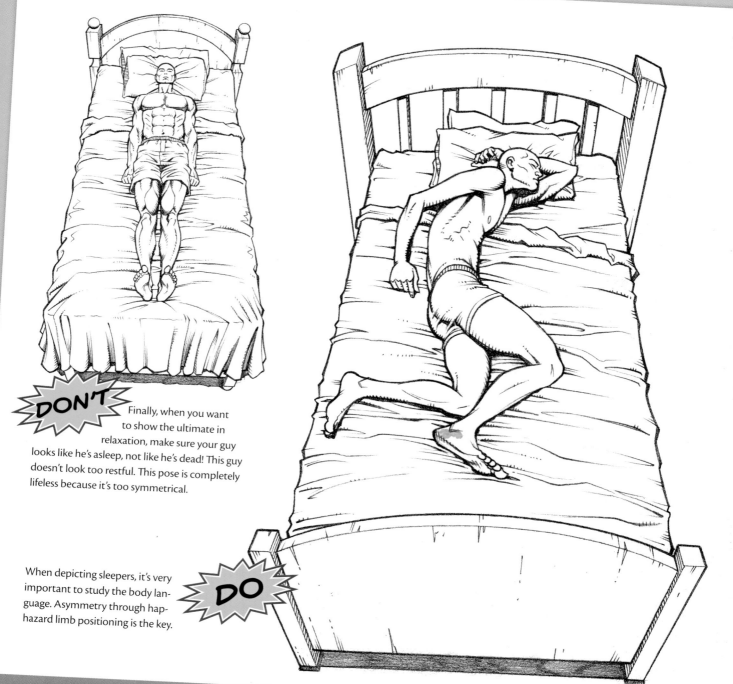

DON'T

Finally, when you want to show the ultimate in relaxation, make sure your guy looks like he's asleep, not like he's dead! This guy doesn't look too restful. This pose is completely lifeless because it's too symmetrical.

When depicting sleepers, it's very important to study the body language. Asymmetry through haphazard limb positioning is the key.

DO

PUMP IT UP!

One trick to show muscularity without all the striations is through the power of veins! Arms are an excellent area to show these spaghettilike strands of oozing power. Don't forget the really big vein right down the middle of the biceps! Sketch them out like a roadmap, then strongly define one side (depending on where your light source is). You can spread veins throughout other parts of the body, too: shoulders, legs, chest—practically anywhere you want! Study bodybuilder magazines to get a sense of their size, flow and direction.

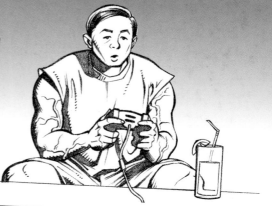

DRAWING WOMEN, BABES, GALS AND KITTENS

Now that we're familiar with drawing the muscle guys, we can move on to those sexy comic book gals! As we did with the stud muffin, we'll first go over some general tips on proportions. Generally, we don't want to depict separate muscles because doing so might masculinize our babes; focus on their simple contours instead. So to begin, here are the basic front, back and side views of our gorgeous gal!

THE FRONT VIEW

Let's keep it simple. The height of a sexy chick in relation to her upper and lower body division is similar to our stud. The major difference is scale; unless you want your women to be the same height or taller than your guys, draw the girls a little shorter and proportionally smaller.

For the males (see pages 14–15), we used the crotch as a landmark to indicate the center of his height, with the distance from crotch to head being equal to the distance from crotch to feet. In the female, the legs from the crotch down should be a little longer than the distance from the head to the crotch, giving her slightly longer, more elegant legs.

THE SIDE VIEW

Remember, when you're looking at the figure from the side, the body isn't aligned in a perfect, straight up-and-down configuration. This especially applies to the ladies because we want to maintain their graceful figures with S-patterns. At least with the guys, you can, at rare times, get away with awkward stiffness.

THE BACK VIEW

The contour of the female's back is identical to the front, as in the male. When the arms are rested, the elbows angle inward just as they are in the front view, there's no reverse effect. Because there is less musculature, there are less contours cutting in front of each other. For the often-confusing placement of back muscles; indicating the shoulder blades and spine will usually do the trick.

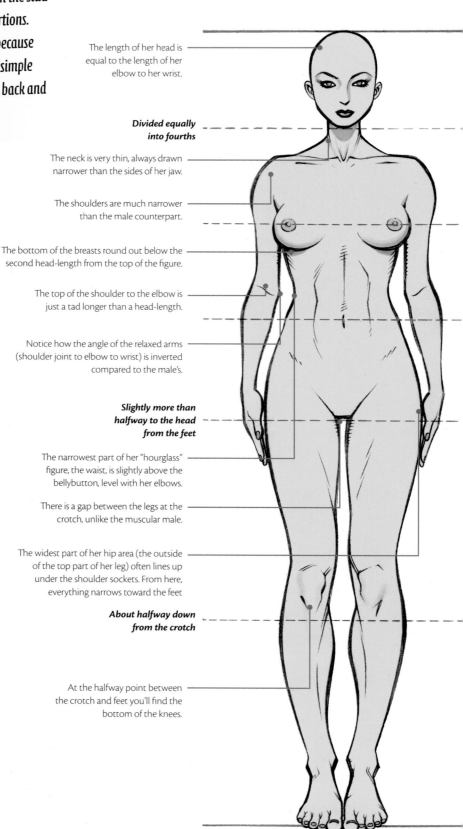

The length of her head is equal to the length of her elbow to her wrist.

Divided equally into fourths

The neck is very thin, always drawn narrower than the sides of her jaw.

The shoulders are much narrower than the male counterpart.

The bottom of the breasts round out below the second head-length from the top of the figure.

The top of the shoulder to the elbow is just a tad longer than a head-length.

Notice how the angle of the relaxed arms (shoulder joint to elbow to wrist) is inverted compared to the male's.

Slightly more than halfway to the head from the feet

The narrowest part of her "hourglass" figure, the waist, is slightly above the bellybutton, level with her elbows.

There is a gap between the legs at the crotch, unlike the muscular male.

The widest part of her hip area (the outside of the top part of her leg) often lines up under the shoulder sockets. From here, everything narrows toward the feet

About halfway down from the crotch

At the halfway point between the crotch and feet you'll find the bottom of the knees.

Unlike the male, there are very few discernable cuts of muscle. Most elements are defined by contour and minimal shading.

The narrow-set shoulder blades are very prominent. There's no muscle mass layer.

Under the breasts, the stomach angles in from the ribcage toward the bellybutton. From there, it will "poof" out again before angling towards the crotch. This is not a gut! It's a natural shape in women! The stomach contour resembles a flattened M.

The neck is thinner, so more of the cranial bulge shows at the back of the head. The back of the neck is much closer to the ear.

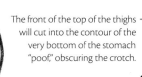

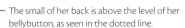

The front of the top of the thighs will cut into the contour of the very bottom of the stomach "poof," obscuring the crotch.

The small of her back is above the level of her bellybutton, as seen in the dotted line.

Prominent "butt dimples" are just below the third head-length down. The tip of the butt crack is below, creating a triangle.

The bottom of the butt flows into the contour of the back of the leg—it doesn't cut into the leg like the male. Avoid a hard angle where the legs begin. Opt for a tight curve.

Unlike the males, the edge of the female buttocks lines up under or extends farther than her upper back. She doesn't carry the muscle in her back to push it out, and the S-curve in her hips and butt is exaggerated. Never draw it more forward than the back!

To maximize the look of tone, draw short buttocks creases. Don't draw them all the way to the edge of the leg.

Like the male, the bottom edge of the buttocks is just below the halfway point of the figure.

The gap between the legs can also be seen from the rear.

The crease on the back of each knee is a little above the halfway point between the buttocks and the feet.

Like the male, the lower leg sits farther back than the upper leg, showing the full effect of the S-shape. Keep her legs thinner, smoother and less defined than her male counterpart!

Keep the length of the foot around the length of the head or smaller. We don't want monster feet on our ladies!

TWO WAYS TO BEGIN

1. First draw the center line that would be her entire length from head to toe. Mark the center point (see page 11). Then take the center point and move it upward just a bit so that the length below (the legs) is a little longer than the length above. Proceed making the necessary divisions to begin drawing.

2. Rough out the upper half of the body (head to crotch), divide it in fourths to establish proper proportions of the head, nipples, and bellybutton. Take a little bit more than that length and add it below the crotch to give yourself the leg length. Proceed with the drawing.

33

THE IMPORTANCE OF S

You're probably sick of hearing this, but I can't stress enough that squiggly S-shapes rule when it comes to drawing babes. And as you'll see, they're used everywhere on their bodies! S-shapes take precedence over muscle definition, so always keep them in mind when you're doing your gesture drawing. Stay loose, light and quick to effectively capture the pose and movement.

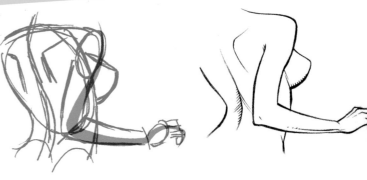

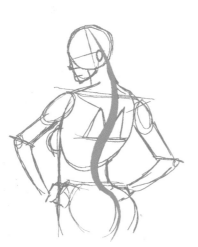
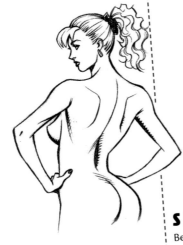

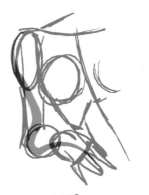
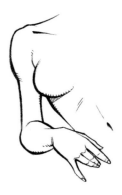

S IN THE ARMS
Believe it or not, a subtle S-shape can also be used in the arms.

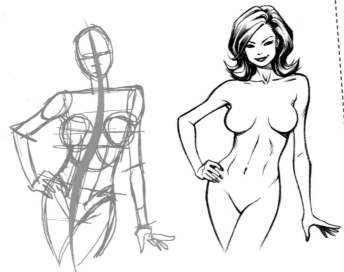

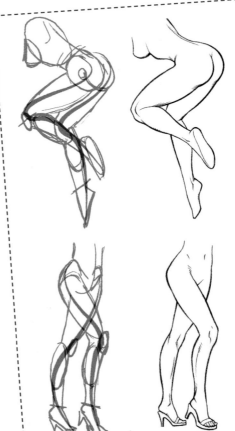

S IN THE HEAD AND TORSO
Use the S-shape to place the head and torso in various positions. Draw it first as the centerline, then build the figure around it.

S IN THE LEGS
S-shapes can appear in the legs too, all the way down to the fee

DON'T BREAK HER!

As much as I've stressed using S-shapes, there is a point where one can take it just a tad too far! Overexaggerating these shapes may result in anatomy that can only be achieved through broken bones and dislocated joints.

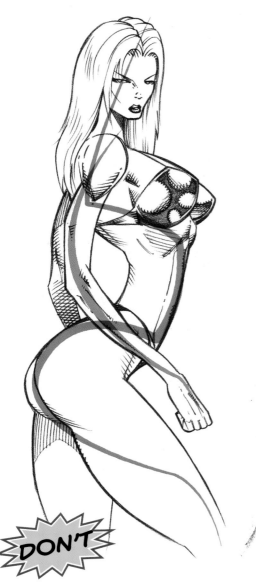

DON'T

Save this girl! Her back seems to be broken and her limbs bent out of shape. She must be in extreme pain! This is an example of how S-shapes can be abused. Especially in the arched back—a common position in superhero stances.

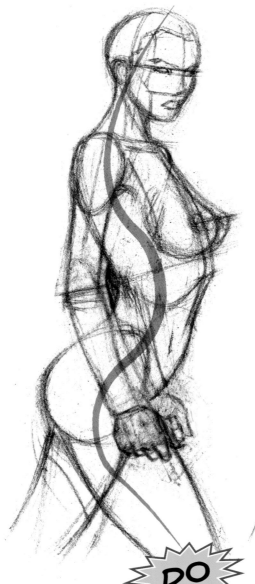

DO

Since the arms and bones are composed of long, straight limbs, keep their S-shapes tamer than when the body is in a straight pose. Draw lightly at first, so if it doesn't look right, you can erase and start over.

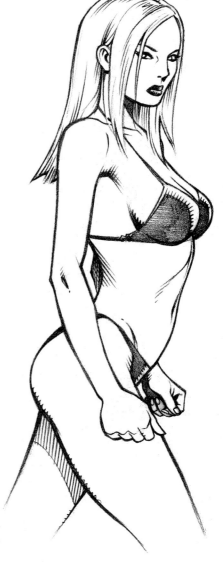

MAKE OR BREAK!

Staying with and taking advantage of the shapes laid down, we see the final rendered drawing of Tay looking more natural, yet still pleasing.

SUCH A PRETTY FACE!

We've already established the general proportions and guidelines for drawing the human head, particularly in the male hero. But what makes a female face feminine?

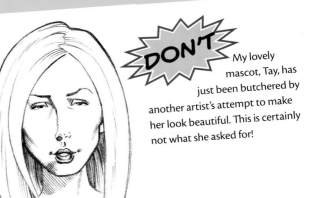

DON'T My lovely mascot, Tay, has just been butchered by another artist's attempt to make her look beautiful. This is certainly not what she asked for!

DEMONSTRATION

FRONT VIEW

The guidelines for proportion and basic divisions are the same for both male and female faces (see page 16). Without further ado, let's go over what will help make your babes' faces very easy on the eyes!

1 SKETCH YOUR BASIC EGG SHAPE
As for the male, divide your shape vertically and horizontally. At this stage, there is essentially no difference between the sexes.

2 ROUGH IN LIGHT FEATURES
First of all, the most important rule when drawing women is that less is more! When you rough in your face, keep it light, simple and curvy—that is, no angular lines in the contour.

3 FINISH CONFIDENTLY
If your proportions are correct, you can finish this drawing confidently. The outline of her face never comes to a sharp point. Keep facial definition to an absolute minimum, if at all. Tay has fuller, beefier lips and eyelashes than a male. Lay off excessive hatching and crosshatching. The eyebrows are simple strokes—not fuzzy caterpillars above her eyes!

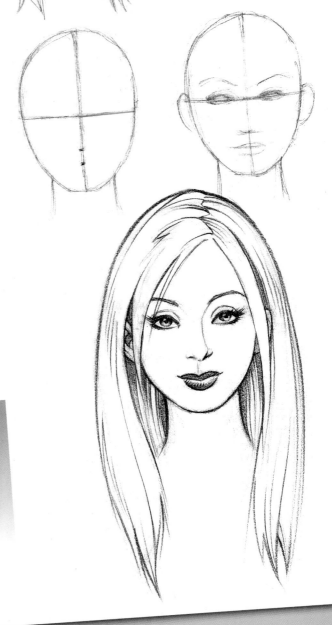

DON'T RUSH!

When you're first learning to draw the female face, don't worry about variation and distinguishing features yet; you're barely able to walk at this point! In trying to learn more advanced techniques too early, you risk making your female faces ugly. Focus on mastering the basic proportions and making the face generically attractive.

SIDE VIEW

The side is still a round circle and a triangular wedge (see page 17). The guidelines remain the same as for the guy's here too, except you can try to instill an elegant feminity in your curves from the beginning.

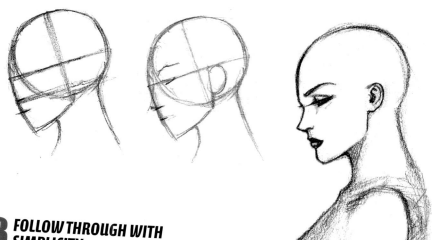

1 DRAW YOUR CIRCLE AND WEDGE

Make the face and jaw for the side view as if you were drawing a male. Add the eye, nose and mouth lines.

2 ROUGH IN THE BASIC FEATURES

Maintain simple, elegant curves throughout this stage.

3 FOLLOW THROUGH WITH SIMPLICITY

Feminize the features with long eyelashes, thin eyebrows, a slightly upturned nose and rounded, "poofier" lips. Don't forget the thin neck.

THREE-QUARTER VIEW

Mark your centerline, which is important for mapping the facial features. From this angle, you would see only one side of the nose.

1 SKETCH YOUR BASIC HEAD

Visualize (and sketch!) your basic head as if it were turned from the front view. The tip of the nose is close to the edge of the face, as are the far eye and lips. For the lips, visualize the centerline running through their center.

2 ADD FEATURES

The far nostril is obscured (you may want to add a drop shadow under the far nostril as shown). Draw more "lippage" on the close side and very little on the far side of the centerline.

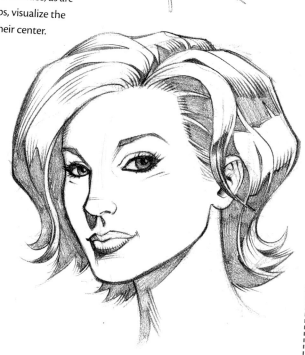

TO RENDER, OR NOT TO RENDER

As much as I stress to avoid rendering in the female face, there are times where it's appropriate—but only if handled delicately! For example, if there are big shadows that are fading from a light source, it's OK to throw out some hatching from the blacks as long as you don't allow them to creep too far into the lighted, smooth areas of the face. This works best if you have to draw a face very large. Rendering at a small scale will only muddy up your drawing.

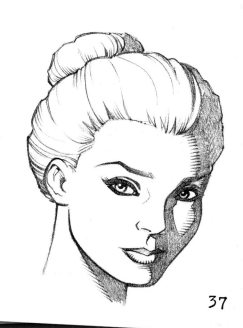

EYES AND NOSE

It's very common and easy to draw the same facial features over and over for different women. But it's boring, and will prevent you from growing as an artist. We recognize individuals because their features are all unique (really, they are). Let's begin with those to-die-for eyes and nose.

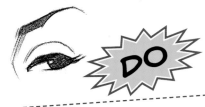

EYES

Avoid drawing individual eyelashes and eyebrow hairs on your women. Remember, we want to get away with as few lines as possible! How do we do this? By using a thick, simple stroke to give the illusion of hairs clumped together. This is a much more effective way to draw pretty eyes.

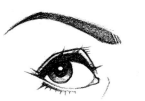

WHY ... HELLO THERE

In women, the eyebrows, eyelashes and eyelids can be modified in many different ways without sacrificing beauty (although you want to keep the upper eyelashes thick). It's common to see big, bedroom eyelids drawn on females. They're attractive, but small or even missing eyelids can be just as alluring.

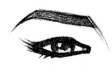
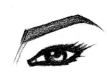

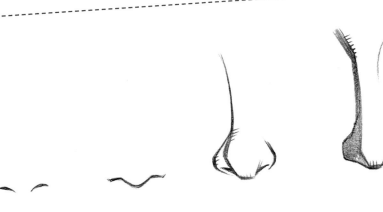
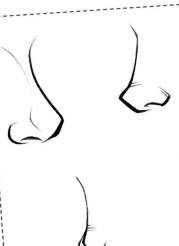

NOSES

This is a very difficult area for many beginners to draw on women. There are several ways to draw female noses:
- draw just the nostrils
- draw only the bottom edge of the nose (flattened U- or M-shape)
- indicate only one side of the nose bridge
- show one nostril in shadow

THE RIGHT TOOL FOR SNUBBING

A prominent line on one side usually will do fine, but at times you may want to add a thin line on the other side. The key is to keep the nose elegant and not overrendered with meaningless dots and dashes.

LIPS

In general, the rule is that women will have big, full lips while the guys will have that area toned down. But do realize that there are attractive women with thin lips (or practically no upper lip!), and guys with thicker lips. Some people have tiny mouths, and others have mouths that seem to stretch from ear to ear. Natural "frowns" might show in one person's facial expression while another's mouth might look upturned as in a smile. Looking at the mouths by themselves, the one factor that usually distinguishes the sexes is that comic book women's lips tend to be a little more heavily shaded (darker) than those of their male counterparts. In fact, it could be argued that the lips are the one area where it's OK for women to have more lines drawn in than the fellas.

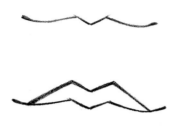

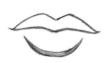

Bolder lip outline

More rendering—but don't go overboard!

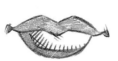

Darkened upper lip with a highlighted lower lip

LIPS

There are three common ways to indicate lips. Generally, the upper lip should form somewhat of an M-shape, with the lower lip drawn thicker. Often, you will see lips emphasized as if they were wearing lipstick.

1 THE M-SHAPE
As with the guys, establish the "M" shape of your choice for the bottom edge of the upper lip. Start in the middle and branch out. This "M" shape is a little more exaggerated in females.

2 UPPER LIP
Draw the upper "M" shape, but this time feel free to make it much bolder and thicker than its male counterpart.

3 LOWER LIP
Draw the lower lip with the same thickness or thicker than the upper lip—never thinner! Heavy darks will indicate a bold and dark lipstick color. The lower lip will catch more light than the upper.

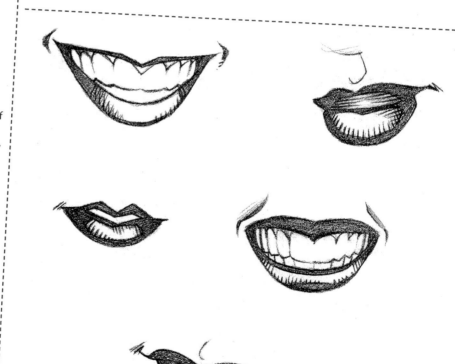

LUSCIOUS AND LOVELY
Here are examples of our ladies' lips. As you did for the man, vary the teeth and the amount of gums showing.

GIVE HAIR SOME SHAPE

A woman's hair is one of the harder things to draw. Hair is daunting enough as it is without the seemingly infinite hairstyles! The biggest problem for newbies is that they see hair as millions of individual strands, which can be very intimidating. Train your eye to capture the essence of hair. Here's a way to make it a little easier!

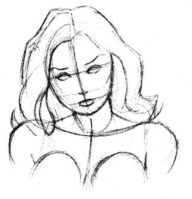

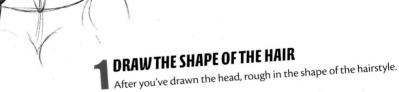

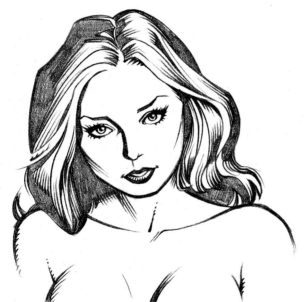

DON'T The hair drawn here is stringy and flat. The typical beginner will draw every strand from the root to the end, because this is what the artist mentally "sees." The result is lifeless and undesirable.

1 DRAW THE SHAPE OF THE HAIR
After you've drawn the head, rough in the shape of the hairstyle.

2 VIEW THE HAIR AS A SOLID MASS
Squint your eyes and imagine the hair as a solid mass, like a slab of rock in the shape of a hairstyle. Now notice where the light source is located. Establish where the highlights and shadows would fall on the mass of hair to describe its form.

3 FINISH THE DRAWING
Add solid lines, with more and thicker lines in the shadow areas you previously established. Leave the highlights free of lines. It's OK to bring a few stray strands from the darks into the highlights to make it interesting.

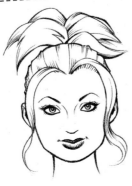

Blond Hair
Stay light on the lines! Obviously, there'll be more light areas than dark. Draw only a few lines in shadow areas.

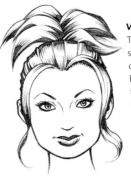

Medium-Toned Hair
Use more lines and even some blacks. Here's a trick: Fade lines from the roots out and from the ends in. This leaves a natural highlight in between to create volume. Add thicker lines or black into similar curves within the hair.

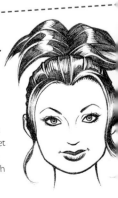

Very Dark or Black Hair
Treat the highlights as squiggly strips of white on a curved, black mass. From these strips, feel free to indicate a few white lines shooting out along the hair's shape. Let the darkness dominate. Represent the roots with short feathering.

GIVE HAIR SOME STYLE

When dealing with real world situations, you want to reflect hairstyles that are trendy for a given time period. Big hair was popular in the 80s and early 90s. Such big hair on today's women may seem outdated (though it may come back in the future!). Keep an eye out not only to find out what's popular, but to find other styles besides the typical curly hair, straight hair and ponytail.

NO MATTER WHAT THE STYLE!
Visualize all styles as solid forms with contours and shadows. Remember, start broadly before adding any details (feathering marks, strands and so forth) Once you establish the lights and darks, everything else is cake!

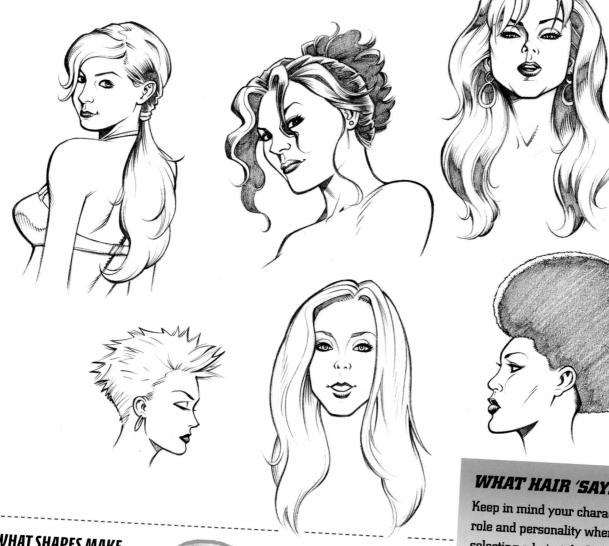

WHAT SHAPES MAKE UP THE HAIR?
Here you can see the solid forms that comes together and form this excited babe.

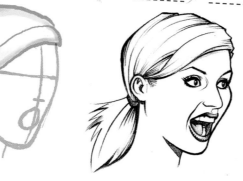

WHAT HAIR 'SAYS'
Keep in mind your character's role and personality when selecting a hairstyle. If your character is active, such as a female martial artist, you may want to keep her hair short or in a ponytail to keep her hair from flying in her face. If she is dark and gothic, dark hair would probably be more suitable than golden blonde.

DRAWING THE FEMALE CHEST

How hard can drawing women's boobs be? Just doodle a couple of big globes sticking out of the chest and voilà—right? If only it were that simple! Nobody likes to look at a badly drawn bust; it would suggest plastic surgery gone wrong! Let's take a closer look at this always-interesting area of a babe and try to understand it better.

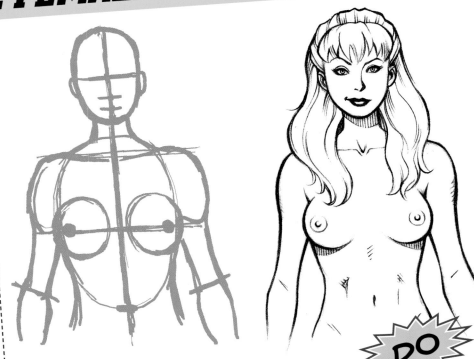

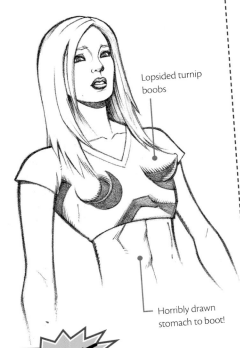

Lopsided turnip boobs

Horribly drawn stomach to boot!

DON'T

Our girl Tay has been drawn with horrible boobs, no matter the angle. The contours are misshapen, and the excessive crosshatching does little to give them appealing form. Unfortunately, she maxed out her credit cards so she can't afford to have them redrawn. Perhaps we can help her?

DO

We know that the nipples would be about a head-length down from the chin (perhaps even a couple of inches higher in comic book land). Mark that off and begin rounding the boobs under this nipple mark. Don't draw the bottom edge of each breast too close to the nipple, or it will look as though the breasts are too high on the chest. Unless she's wearing a top that pushes the boobs inward, leave a gap between them. Avoid rounding the inside edges of the breasts (near the sternum) too high—this looks unnatural. When tightening, give some "weight" by adding line thickness at the bottom curves. Taper them into thin lines as they curve up. Don't render any further, unless maybe you want minimal feathering at the bottom edges.

THE MANY MOODS OF BOOBS

Think about how different situations and positions affect the shape of the breast. In a reclining position, the breast tissue flattens and spreads out due to gravity. If the girl is upside-down, the breast will push toward her chin. This is a case where the top will have a convex shape.

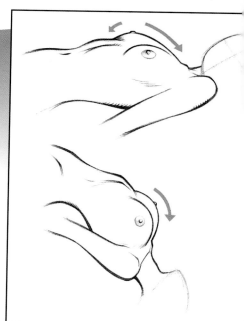

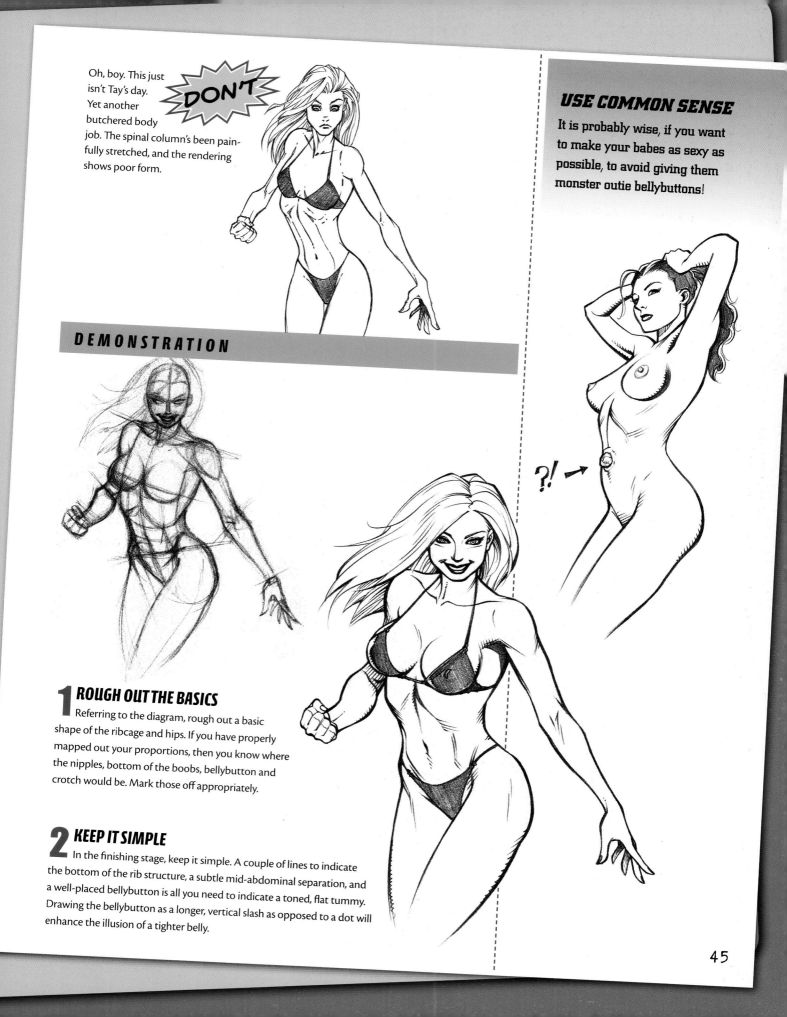

Oh, boy. This just isn't Tay's day. Yet another butchered body job. The spinal column's been painfully stretched, and the rendering shows poor form.

DON'T

It is probably wise, if you want to make your babes as sexy as possible, to avoid giving them monster outie bellybuttons!

DEMONSTRATION

?!→

1 ROUGH OUT THE BASICS
Referring to the diagram, rough out a basic shape of the ribcage and hips. If you have properly mapped out your proportions, then you know where the nipples, bottom of the boobs, bellybutton and crotch would be. Mark those off appropriately.

2 KEEP IT SIMPLE
In the finishing stage, keep it simple. A couple of lines to indicate the bottom of the rib structure, a subtle mid-abdominal separation, and a well-placed bellybutton is all you need to indicate a toned, flat tummy. Drawing the bellybutton as a longer, vertical slash as opposed to a dot will enhance the illusion of a tighter belly.

HIPS, SHOULDERS, BELLYBUTTONS

Pay attention to the hip-to-shoulder relationship. It will keep your pretty babes from twisting out of their own bodies.

Since simplicity is key, get used to using things (shading, white space) other than lines to get your point across.

➡ Here, the hips and shoulders are tipped in the same direction. (We won't even mention the horribly drawn stomach.) The result is an unattractive figure thrown off balance.

➡➡ The lines of the shoulders and the hips should be tipped at opposing angles to create counterbalance. This results in a more natural look.

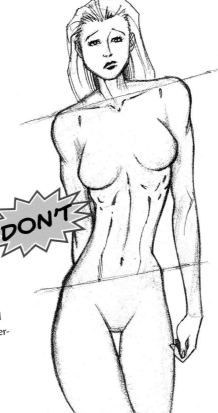

DON'T

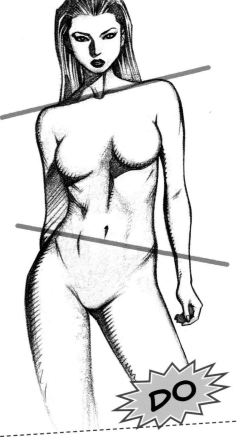

DO

TAKE ADVANTAGE OF HER SHADOWS

If you are using a reference photo with dramatic lighting, squint your eyes and try to see the shapes of the light areas and the dark areas in relation to each other. Take advantage of well-placed shadows to create form; the mind's eye will fill in the rest.

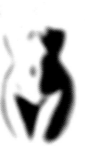

Start squinting to see the black areas!

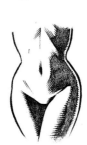

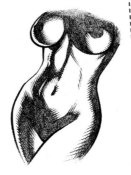

A LITTLE DAB WILL DO YA

Sometimes all you need is a simple bellybutton to get your point across. If in doubt, avoid overrendering and focus on the contour of the waist.

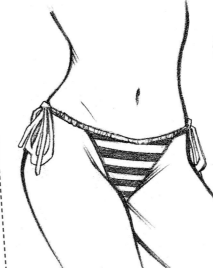

KEEP IT SIMPLE, STUPID!

As I've already mentioned, the key to drawing women is to keep it simple. It's easy enough to throw too many lines on male superheroes, and you may even be able to get away with that at times. But drawing pretty ladies is a delicate venture; one line in the wrong place can spell disaster! Focus on good structure and contouring; the rest will take care of itself.

DEMONSTRATION

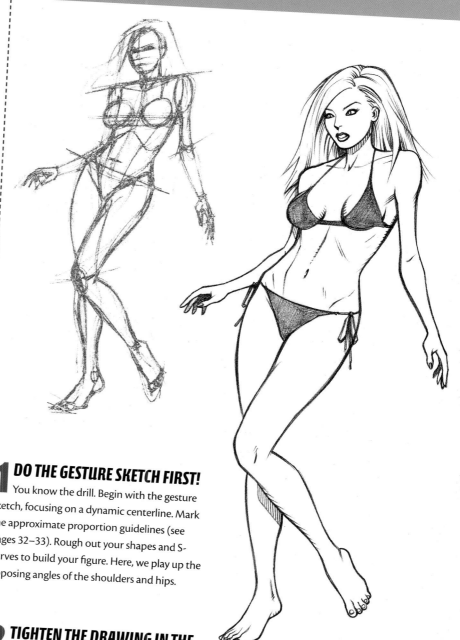

1 DO THE GESTURE SKETCH FIRST!

You know the drill. Begin with the gesture sketch, focusing on a dynamic centerline. Mark the approximate proportion guidelines (see pages 32–33). Rough out your shapes and S-curves to build your figure. Here, we play up the opposing angles of the shoulders and hips.

2 TIGHTEN THE DRAWING IN THE RIGHT PLACES

See the difference between the first example and this one? Fewer lines, used only in the right places. When it comes to drawing hot babes, less is more—*keep it simple!*

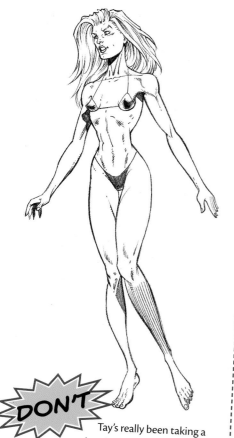

DON'T

Tay's really been taking a beating, hasn't she? This is another artist's overrendered interpretation in an attempt to make the drawing "detailed." It seems as if extra lines are used to make up for poor gesture and to hide anatomical problems.

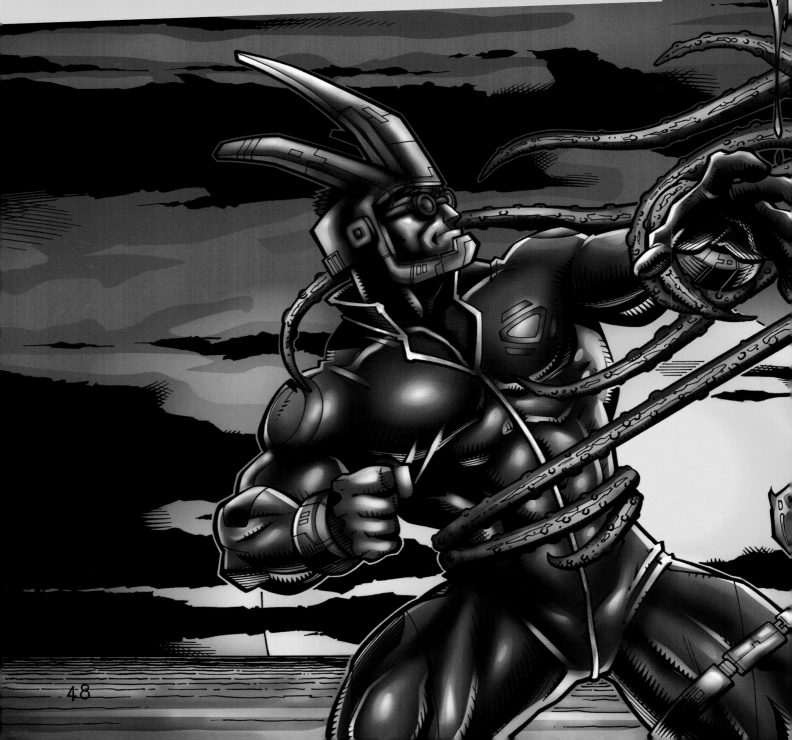

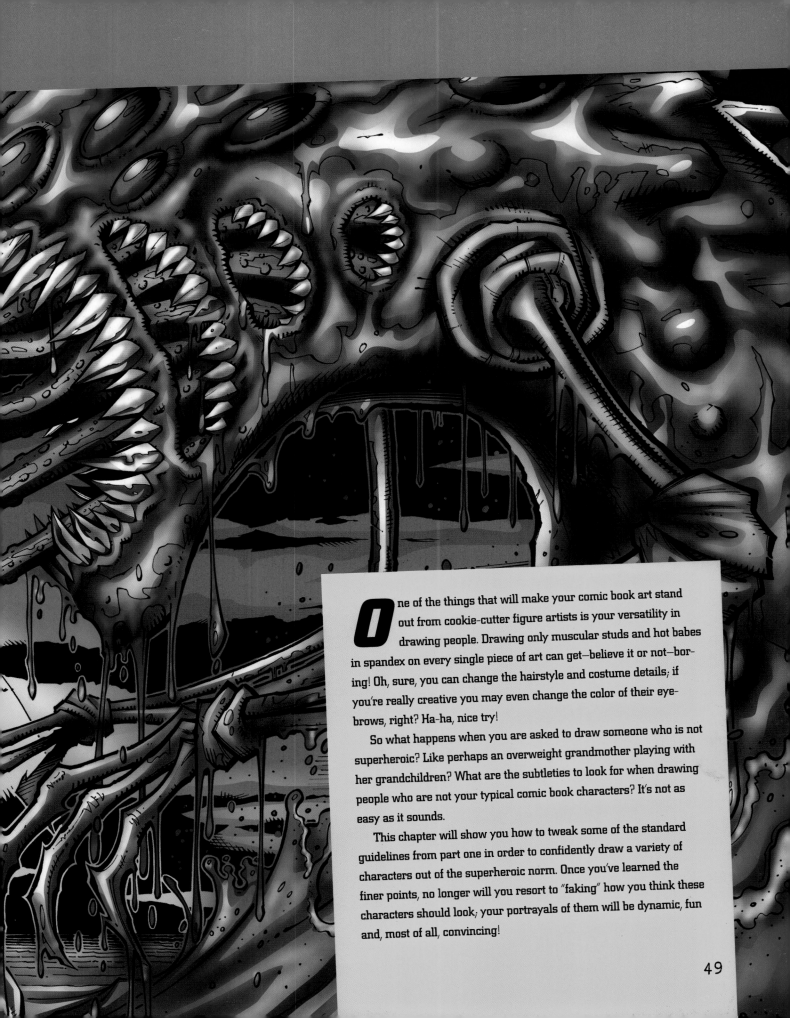

One of the things that will make your comic book art stand out from cookie-cutter figure artists is your versatility in drawing people. Drawing only muscular studs and hot babes in spandex on every single piece of art can get—believe it or not—boring! Oh, sure, you can change the hairstyle and costume details; if you're really creative you may even change the color of their eyebrows, right? Ha-ha, nice try!

So what happens when you are asked to draw someone who is not superheroic? Like perhaps an overweight grandmother playing with her grandchildren? What are the subtleties to look for when drawing people who are not your typical comic book characters? It's not as easy as it sounds.

This chapter will show you how to tweak some of the standard guidelines from part one in order to confidently draw a variety of characters out of the superheroic norm. Once you've learned the finer points, no longer will you resort to "faking" how you think these characters should look; your portrayals of them will be dynamic, fun and, most of all, convincing!

TALES OF THE WEIRD AND SKINNY

STRANGE MELON DUDE!

Let's start with head shapes. We're now venturing into a more cartoony world with our artwork, but that's not to say that we can't use these elements in comic book art.

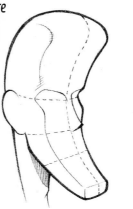
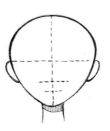
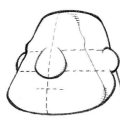
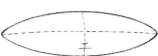

LIMITLESS SHAPES

Just about any shape you can imagine can be used as a head shape to create unique characters. The shapes can be geometric, lopsided, horizontally or vertically oriented. Just keep in mind the dimensionality of these shapes: imagine how they would look from different angles and turned in different directions so that your character can look consistent no matter the viewpoint.

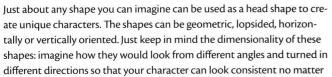
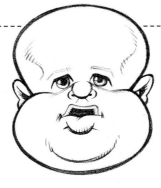
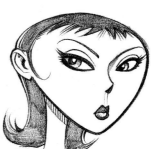
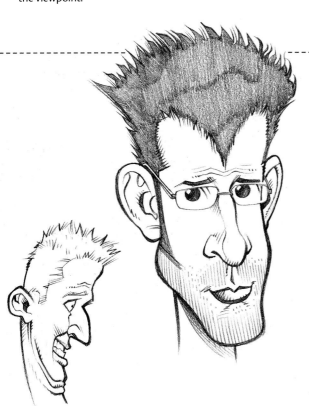
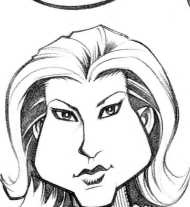
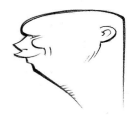

LIMITLESS HEADS

Playing around with different head shapes yields different heads. When we're dealing with more cartoony heads, the rules of proportion needn't apply. For example, the eye line doesn't necessarily have to divide the head into equal upper and lower halves.

SKIN AND BONES

Messing around with body types will help you avoid drawing cookie-cutter characters all the time. Here, we'll look at the extremely skinny figure.

Drawing "skinny" is not just about stretching out the trunk and limbs until they're thin; it's about playing down muscle bulges and focusing on bony protrusions as well.

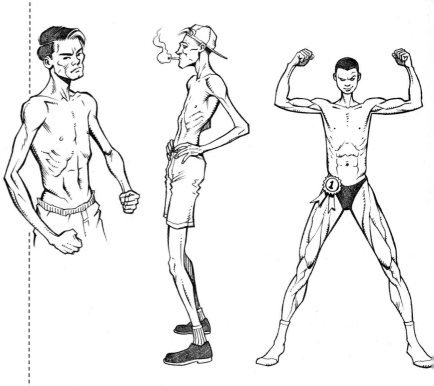

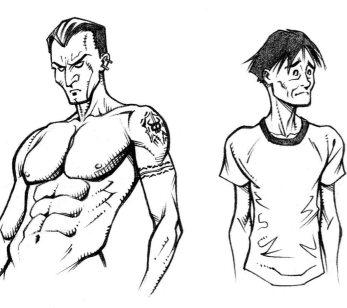

WHAT'S IT TAKE TO BE SKIN AND BONES?

Notice the presence of bony structures such as the cheekbones, ribs, collarbones, wrists and hips. It's almost as if there were just a thin layer of skin on top of bone, with very little muscle.

GIMME YOUR LUNCH MONEY!

Note the "coat hanger" shoulders and wiry neck on the guys. No beefy wrestlers here!

LEAN AND NOT SO MEAN

Skinny guys are skinny not only because they lack big muscle, but also because they have very little fat. Lean people tend to have more veins showing, so play up the veins to enhance the thin effect.

THE SPICE OF LIFE?

It's more common to see males drawn with exaggerated body types in comics. Not that there's anything wrong with messing around with female figures, but comic books like to show off the sexy girl more often than, um ... the others.

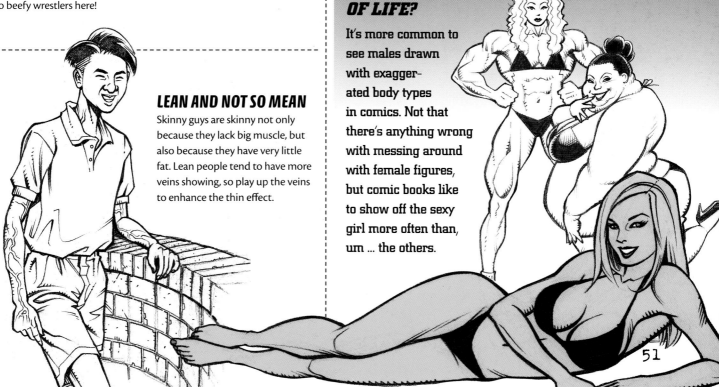

TALES OF THE JUST PLAIN HUGE

I'M JUST BIG BONED

Heavy bodies are actually much easier to draw than you think. You only have to deal with round curves, thick appendages, and practically no muscle definition (so no need to memorize your anatomy!). Just be careful where you choose to put your lines of definition (or lack of definition, rather).

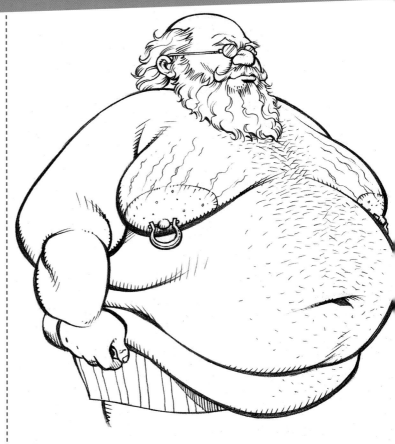

A typical way some artists draw an obese male. The contouring is way too sculpted, creating a mismatch between lean musculature and dense fat in the same body. The neck is clearly separated from the head here—a fatty no-no.

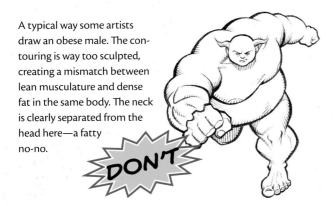

DON'T

Keep your shapes very round and smooth, like a detailed snowman. In the roughing stage, draw your basic oval and circle shapes overlapping each other (draw through). Bisect some of those shapes to get a midline.

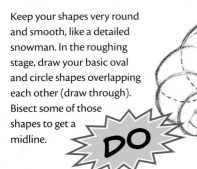

DO

TIGHTEN ... OR SHOULD I SAY FLABBEN?

Don't sculpt any musculature! Keep your lines flowing and curved; elbow joints and knee joints are nonexistent. "Smush" the head onto the rest of the body. For effect, I drew man-boobs flopping away while the gentleman is in motion.

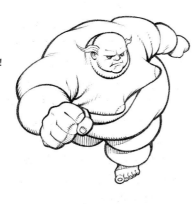

FATTIES' BOOBS ARE A SEXLESS AFFLICTION

They just aren't the same! These are large, stretched-out, stretch-*marked* man-boobs hanging off to the side as opposed to straight down. Pepperoni nipples close to the bottom edge (if not *at* the bottom edge!) show the pull.

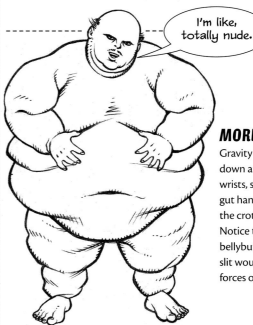

I'm like, totally nude.

MORE ROLLS!

Gravity pulls the fat down around the elbows, wrists, stomach (the gut hangs right over the crotch!) and calves. Notice the slit where the bellybutton is; a vertical slit wouldn't show the forces of gravity.

HYPER-MUSCULAR

If you've practiced some of the anatomy lessons from this book, this part should be fairly easy. Basically, you want to exaggerate the bulges and striations in your dude. Avoid lengthening the limbs and torso to accomodate extra muscle—this defeats the purpose of drawing extreme muscularity.

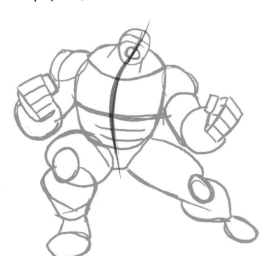

SQUAT BODY AND SHRUNKEN HEAD

One way to portray extreme muscle is to draw your figures very squat with thick joints. It also helps to shrink the head to a smaller-than-normal proportion, so your figure won't look short. Small joints at the elbows, wrists, knees and ankles give the impression of hard-earned muscle on a once-skinny frame. But always, always start with a centerline!

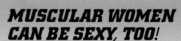

THE POWER OF VEINS

You can't have tons of muscle without veins! Rough out your muscle separations first, then draw noodlelike veins on top (lightly!). Add details with a light source in mind, consistently darkening a side for dimension.

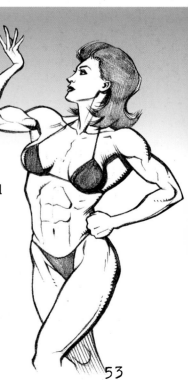

MUSCULAR WOMEN CAN BE SEXY, TOO!

It's easy to draw a muscular male body, then add boobs and a girl's face. But what about the subtle muscles of a very toned, yet still attractive, woman? Go easy on the lines. Focus more on character and soft angles in the contours of the arms, hips and legs (e.g. more of a "dent" where the deltoid meets the arm). Draw a six-pack if you want, but keep the lines thin so the muscles don't look too carved-in. Veins, if any, should be limited to the biceps.

53

DRAWING KIDS AND TEENAGERS

When you think of creating comic books, drawing kids isn't exactly first on your list. You'd rather draw muscular heroes and sexy, cunning vixens, right? But if you want to take comic book art seriously, learn to be versatile in your abilities.

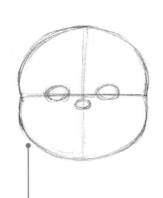

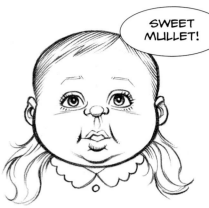

SWEET MULLET!

UM, YEAH ... A REAL CUTIE

Look at the relationship between the eyes and the nose in this baby. See how the small, underdeveloped nose is pushed waaaay up—almost right between the eyes? As the nose is pushed up, draw the gap between the nose and mouth even wider. Make the eyes huge in relation to the head. And don't even think about adding cheekbones!

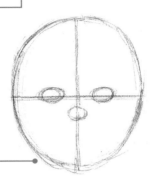

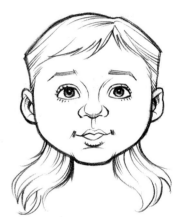

STILL BRIGHT-EYED

A typical preteen kid. Drop the nose down a little, but keep it small and somewhat high. Draw the eyes big but add a head full of hair. Avoid definition in the cheek structure, and maintain the head's smooth and curvy contour.

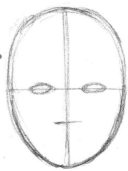
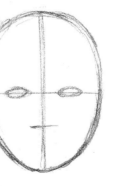

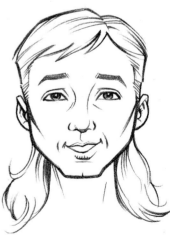

PARENTS JUST DON'T UNDERSTAND

Here we have a mid-teenager. Drop his nose to just about the normal adult level. Keep the eyes subtly bigger. Draw his facial contour with some signs of form, including faint indications of cheek structure. Keep extra hard angles, detail and crosshatching to a minimum.

ALL GROWN UP!

Our little tyke has become a man (*sniff*). Notice how the proportions have changed over all these years.

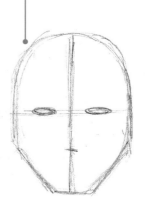

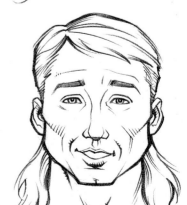

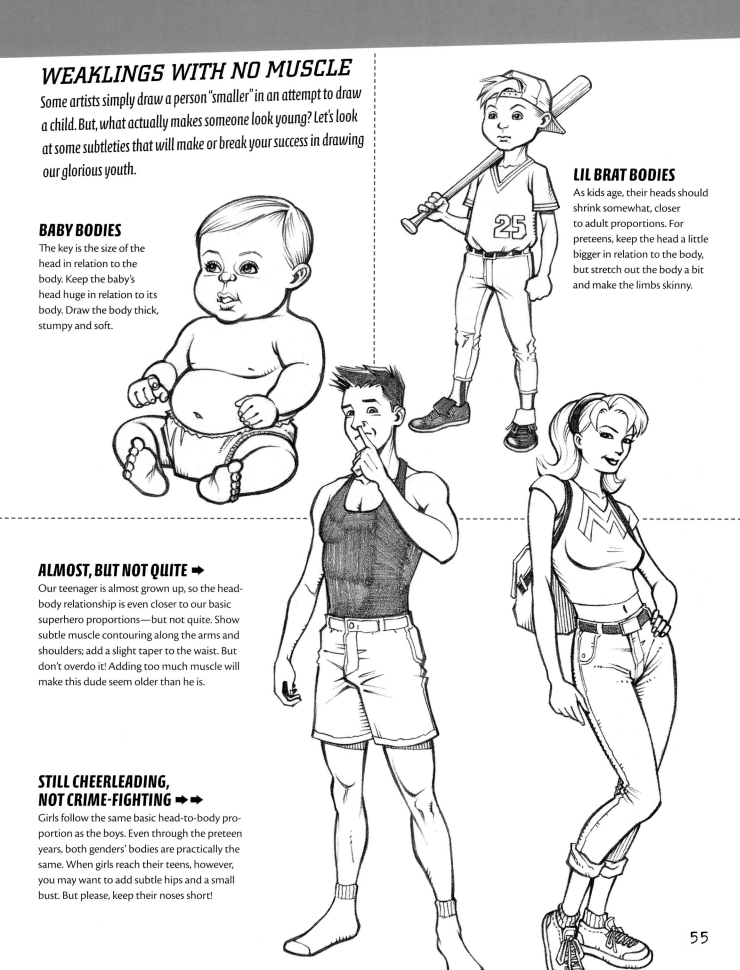

WEAKLINGS WITH NO MUSCLE

Some artists simply draw a person "smaller" in an attempt to draw a child. But, what actually makes someone look young? Let's look at some subtleties that will make or break your success in drawing our glorious youth.

BABY BODIES

The key is the size of the head in relation to the body. Keep the baby's head huge in relation to its body. Draw the body thick, stumpy and soft.

LIL BRAT BODIES

As kids age, their heads should shrink somewhat, closer to adult proportions. For preteens, keep the head a little bigger in relation to the body, but stretch out the body a bit and make the limbs skinny.

ALMOST, BUT NOT QUITE ➡

Our teenager is almost grown up, so the head-body relationship is even closer to our basic superhero proportions—but not quite. Show subtle muscle contouring along the arms and shoulders; add a slight taper to the waist. But don't overdo it! Adding too much muscle will make this dude seem older than he is.

STILL CHEERLEADING, NOT CRIME-FIGHTING ➡ ➡

Girls follow the same basic head-to-body proportion as the boys. Even through the preteen years, both genders' bodies are practically the same. When girls reach their teens, however, you may want to add subtle hips and a small bust. But please, keep their noses short!

DRAWING OUR ELDERS

Elderly people are great fun to draw, but some artists have just as difficult a time drawing them as they do children. Drawing the elderly is more than just adding crow's feet at the corners of the eyes. There are unique characteristics that are critical to properly aging a person. Practice portraying the aged to maximize your skills in drawing facial variety.

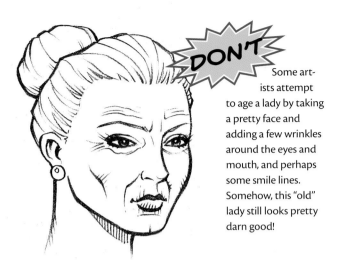

DON'T

Some artists attempt to age a lady by taking a pretty face and adding a few wrinkles around the eyes and mouth, and perhaps some smile lines. Somehow, this "old" lady still looks pretty darn good!

THE GOLDEN YEARS
Notice the seemingly limitless variety in elderly men and women.

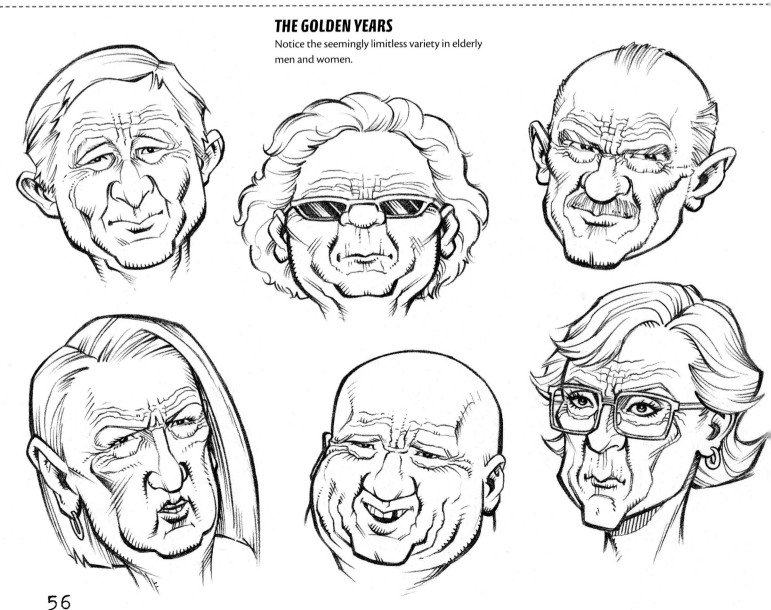

You must really observe the individual facial features in detail.

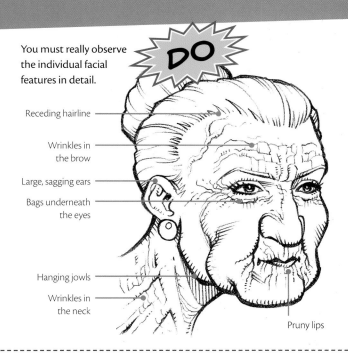

DO

- Receding hairline
- Wrinkles in the brow
- Large, sagging ears
- Bags underneath the eyes
- Hanging jowls
- Wrinkles in the neck
- Pruny lips

BAGS OF BONES

With all due respect, it would be very unusual to portray old people in comics as powerful superheroes. What comes to mind when you describe how they look? Tired? Grumpy? Frail? OK, let's not get ourselves into deeper trouble! The point is to show these adjectives with body language.

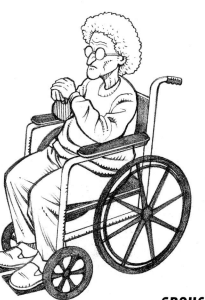

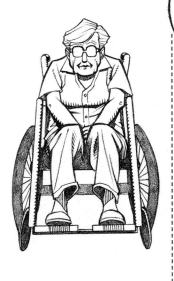

GROUCHES ON WHEELS
Or you could take the easy way out by drawing the elderly in wheelchairs!

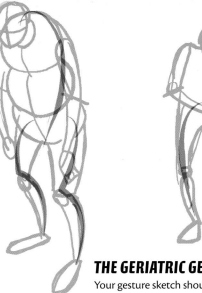

THE GERIATRIC GESTURE
Your gesture sketch should be dynamic and exaggerated. In this example, it almost seems as though our old guy has a look of defeat and fatigue. Play up the hunched back—that's key! Draw bent knees to complement the "old" look. Keep the arms hanging lifelessly at the sides to convey weariness.

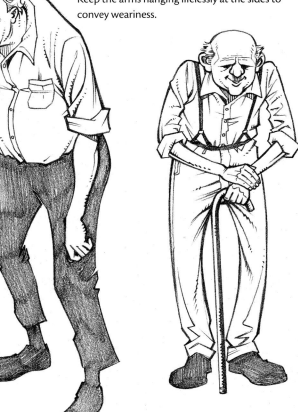

GET AWAY KID, YA BOTHER ME!
Finish your drawing, having fun with the facial features, attire and props to suit your elder's needs.

JOY

We learned about individual facial features; now let's put them to good use by involving them in facial expressions.

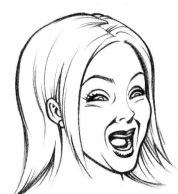

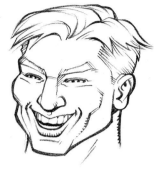

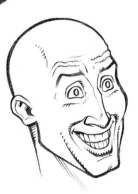

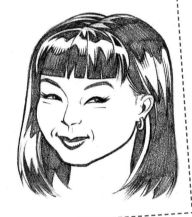

YAY!

Smiles are a necessity when portraying happiness or laughter. They can be open- or closed-mouth. Laugh lines appear as the mouth corners are upturned (whether wide open or not). Eyes can be big or squinty. Often the eyebrows are raised.

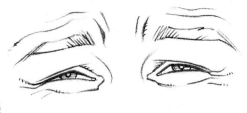

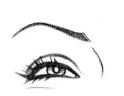

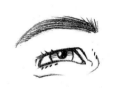

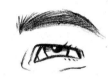

THINGS ARE LOOKING UP!

Notice how the lower eyelids are pushed up when there is an expression of joy.

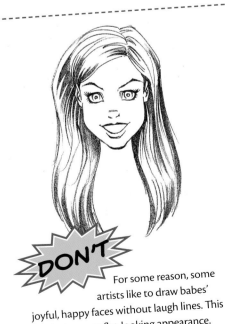

DON'T

For some reason, some artists like to draw babes' joyful, happy faces without laugh lines. This results in a very flat-looking appearance.

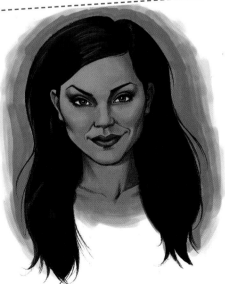

DONE!

Sometimes artists have trouble rendering a realistic expression in comic book art for fear of aging the face. In more realistic art, they seem to have no problem.

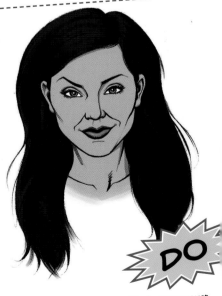

DO

In comic art, lines are simplified, so you must choose them carefully. For the smile, keep them thin, smooth and clean to maintain feminine attractiveness.

SADNESS

Naturally, if we have happiness, then we must also deal with its opposite. Check out the different ways sadness can be shown.

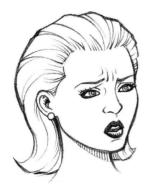
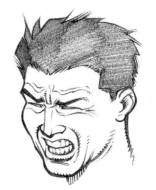
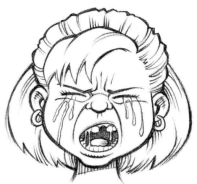

MORE THAN A FROM

The eyes alone can tell the whole story. Whether you want tears or not, pay close attention to the shape of the eyelids as the brow furrows upward. The furrowing pushes into the eyelids, changing their shape. Notice the different mouth shapes as well.

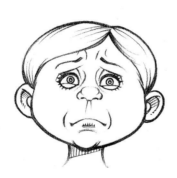
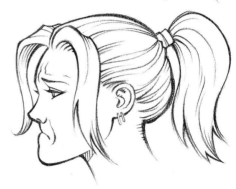

EVERYTHING'S FINE HERE

Here is a set of eyes in their normal state ...

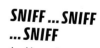

SNIFF ... SNIFF ... SNIFF

And here they are in a saddened state. Notice the eyebrow direction and the eyelids' change in shape. Add tears for additional impact.

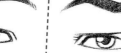

ANGER

Anger is an expression used often in comic book art. That's because there's a lot of conflict between our heroes and villains! Here are some of the many ways to draw an angry face.

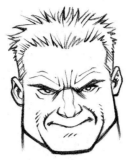
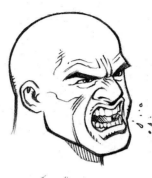
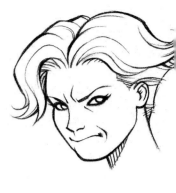

GRRRRRRR!
The one thing in common here is the furrowed brow with meanie eyebrows. This isn't quite the same furrowed brow used in sadness; the eyebrows angle down, also pushing on the upper eyelids to affect the shape of the eyes.

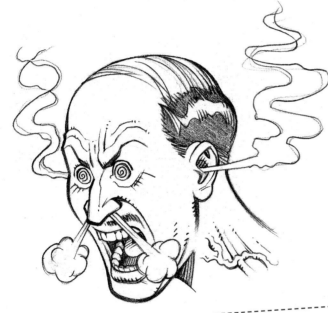
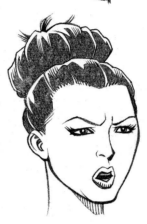
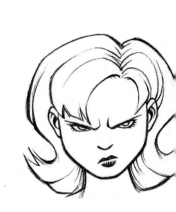

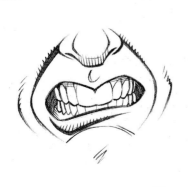
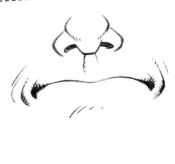
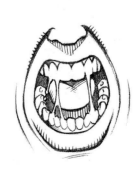
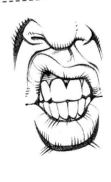

IT'S ALL IN THE MOUTH
Check out the various ways that the mouth can be portrayed in anger. You can have gritted teeth, closed mouth, wide-open mouth, partially open mouth—the list goes on and on.

FRIGHT

Fright is an invaluable expression in comics because there are so many situations that call for it. For instance, someone could be scared by an alien monster jumping out of the trees, a damsel in distress might fear for her life while in captivity, or someone might be on guard while tip-toeing through a haunted house.

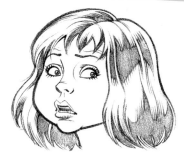
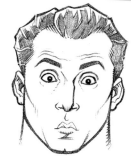

WHAT'S THE MATTER?

The expressions of fright and surprise are closely related; it's the context that helps the viewer identify what the character is feeling. Here are some examples. They can range from apprehension to an outright, open-mouthed scare. Although mouth positions differ, the eyes are always drawn wide and open.

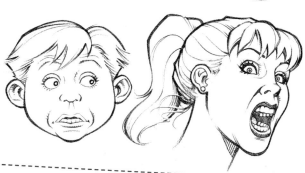

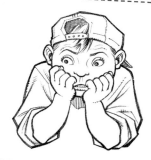
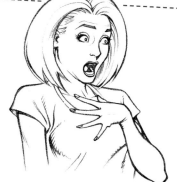

USE YOUR HANDS

Facial expressions aren't the only way to show fright; body language, especially with the hands, can be a great complement to the face. Think of the hands as an accessory in this case: you don't necessarily need them, but they will definitely add more to the overall package.

NORMAL EYES

In a normal state, the eyes have very little character.

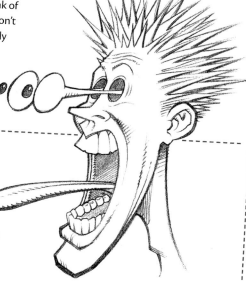

SCARED OUT OF YOUR SKULL

Of course, you can take fright as far as you need to as long as you don't mind a humorous approach. Go all-out nuts if you must!

FRIGHTENED EYES

In fright, the eyebrows lift high and the eyelids follow, allowing the white of the eyes to show all around the iris. You may also see wrinkles in the forehead, but in an all-out scare you'd rarely see the furrow between the eyebrows.

SUPERHERO STYLE

Costumes on our studs and babes can be fairly easy to draw since they tend to favor the skintight variety. After all, what's the point of learning how to draw those bodacious bodies if you can't show them off? Now that we've learned our anatomy, it shouldn't be hard to add the sleeve lines, boots, and a funky design on the body itself to complete the costume.

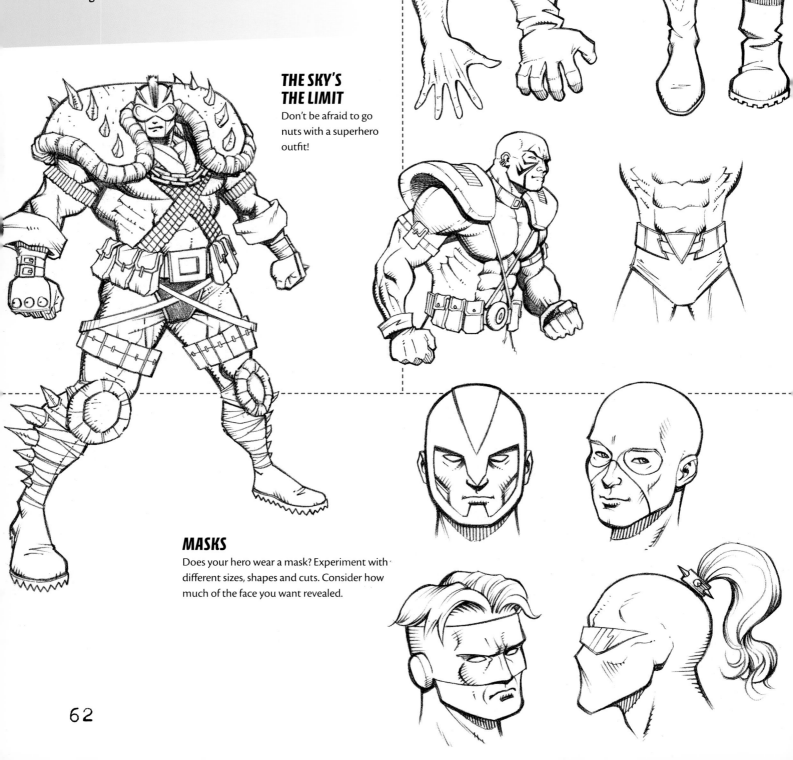

THE SKY'S THE LIMIT
Don't be afraid to go nuts with a superhero outfit!

MASKS
Does your hero wear a mask? Experiment with different sizes, shapes and cuts. Consider how much of the face you want revealed.

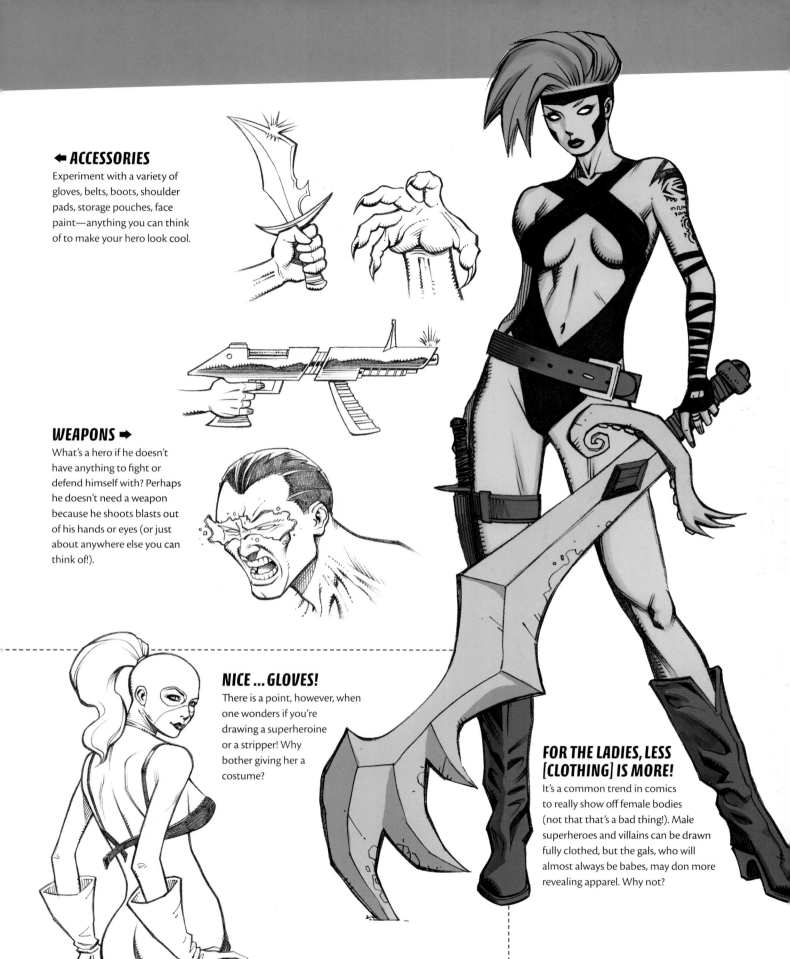

← ACCESSORIES

Experiment with a variety of gloves, belts, boots, shoulder pads, storage pouches, face paint—anything you can think of to make your hero look cool.

WEAPONS →

What's a hero if he doesn't have anything to fight or defend himself with? Perhaps he doesn't need a weapon because he shoots blasts out of his hands or eyes (or just about anywhere else you can think of!).

NICE ... GLOVES!

There is a point, however, when one wonders if you're drawing a superheroine or a stripper! Why bother giving her a costume?

FOR THE LADIES, LESS [CLOTHING] IS MORE!

It's a common trend in comics to really show off female bodies (not that that's a bad thing!). Male superheroes and villains can be drawn fully clothed, but the gals, who will almost always be babes, may don more revealing apparel. Why not?

63

GOING CASUAL

Like it or not, all comic book artists will have to draw regular people at times. Before, we covered physical attributes that can help differentiate superheroes from the average layperson. Now we'll take a closer look at the casual attire that a typical person wears. Regular clothes help ground your characters in reality when you want to take a break from fantasy. After all, you can't draw everyone in spandex all the time!

1 ROUGH OUT THE FIGURE

This is the most important step when drawing any type of clothing over a figure. The way clothes fit and wrinkle depend on the form of the body underneath—not to mention proper figure proportions. Constructing your clothed figure without an accurate understructure will result in a drawing that looks a bit "off."

2 BEGIN THE CLOTHES

Now we can begin roughing in a T-shirt and some jeans on our guy. Pay attention to where the fabric hugs the body and where it hangs away. Because you have the figure roughed out underneath the clothes, you can confidently show where the sleeves, waistband, collar and everything else begin and end.

3 FINISH CONFIDENTLY

Use bold, confident lines. Pay close attention to where there are wrinkles and folds: the armpit area, the crotch area and at the bottom of the pants where the fabric bunches up. Use references if you need them to accurately draw wrinkles.

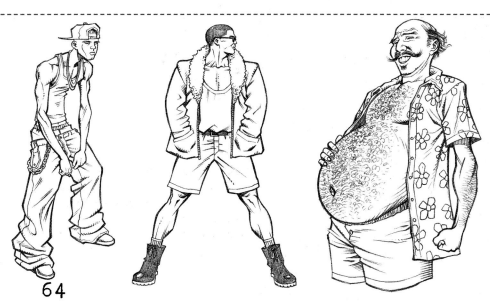

TAKIN' HER EASY!

Here are some examples of other outfits you can draw on a male. It doesn't hurt to stray from the usual. Have fun creating different types of clothing, as well as how it is worn.

64

1 ROUGH OUT THE FIGURE

Start with a simple female figure. Follow the same rules as the guys when you are drawing them. Remember that women's clothing tends to have a little more variety and can be more form-fitting to show off their bodies.

2 LAY IN THE CLOTHING

Decide what you want the young lady to wear. Here, we'll give our girl a cute but casual hooded shirt, jean skirt and platform shoes.

3 CLEAN AND FINISH

Erasing away the initial sketch lines may make them feel like a waste of effort. But it's well worth it when the finished product shows the figure underneath the clothing. Roughing in the clothing without forming the figure first makes the understructure less believable.

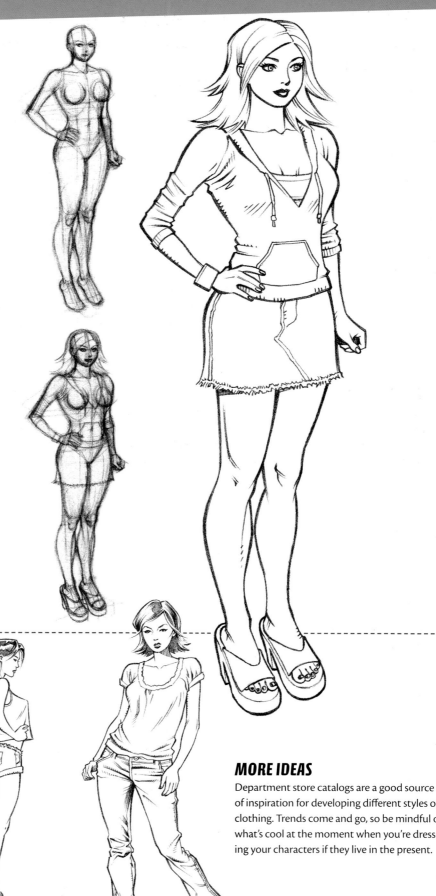

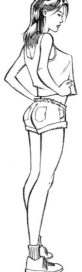

MORE IDEAS

Department store catalogs are a good source of inspiration for developing different styles of clothing. Trends come and go, so be mindful of what's cool at the moment when you're dressing your characters if they live in the present.

STEPPIN' OUT

While we're on the subject of regular folks, we may as well cover formal clothing. The first thing that comes to my mind when thinking about styles for big events and weddings is definitely not T-shirts and jeans. Ever notice how formal clothes always seem to be so clean and free of excessive wrinkles (unless they're obviously bunched up or at a bent joint), especially in photos and catalogs? Photographers always like to make sure there are as few unnatural wrinkles as possible to show the elegance of formal clothing. And that clean elegance is one thing you should keep in mind here.

1 START WITH THE FIGURE
You know the routine by now: we start by sketching the basic shapes of our handsome guy before we dress him up for his wedding.

2 BEGIN THE CLOTHES
Let's give our guy a nice tuxedo—complete with a bow tie, cummerbund and dress shoes. Heck, let's give him preppie glasses while we're at it. Note the counterbalanced lines of the shoulders in relation to the hips. The knee, however, will mimic the angle of the hips.

3 CLEAN AND READY
In the final version, we see our guy all cleaned up and ready for his big event. We can also see that when dealing with dress coats, the thicker fabric prevents excessive, tiny wrinkling throughout most of the trunk. Naturally, the fabric is bunched up on our guy's right arm where it is slightly raised and bent at the elbow.

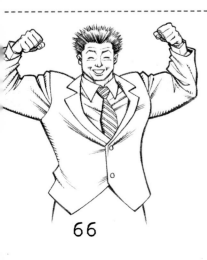
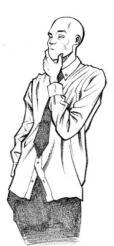
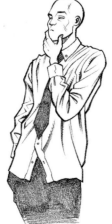
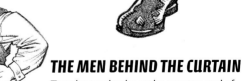

THE MEN BEHIND THE CURTAIN
Tuxedos tend to be at the very top end of formal attire, and generally they aren't common enough to draw on a regular basis. Formal wear can also include looks for the businessman. These clothes include different ties, button-up shirts and vests.

1 ROUGH IN THE FIGURE

Women's formal wear seems to have a lot more variety. This can make their clothing much more interesting to draw than a typical guy's. Here, we'll once again begin with roughing in the curvy, elegant shapes of our lovely young lady. What she is doing is beyond me, but it seems she's in motion.

2 LAY IN THE CLOTHES

We are giving this woman a nice flowing gown. Don't worry about covering up the figure with the clothes, particularly the legs. They'll help you know how long the skirt should be coming off her hips and butt. Add a slit to the dress to show off that back leg you've worked so hard to rough in. Feel free to add a showy necklace and bracelets.

3 CLEAN AND SIMPLIFY

The final drawing is very clean to complement the simplicity of the gown. Avoid excessive crosshatching in both the figure and the outfit—a double-whammy of avoidance! I lengthened the dress just a bit, and added a shadow under the skirt to ground the young lady. After all, there is no way light can shine from in there, and the only light getting in is through the slit.

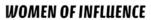

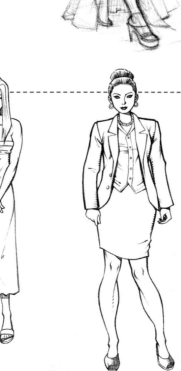

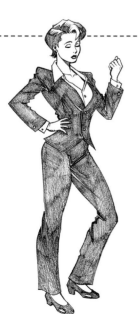

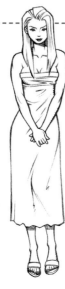

WOMEN OF INFLUENCE

Like men's tuxedos, women's gowns and dresses are worn on only the special occasions. Here are some more average applications of women's formal wear. Choosing styles to fit the situation is the key.

SHOES, HATS AND GLOVES

Just as they can spruce up superhero costumes, items such as shoes and hats can add flair to everyday outfits. Although you may dress your characters as you wish, accessories should make sense with the rest of their clothing, the season of the year and the setting of the story. Observe details and consider what makes one style different from another.

THE MANY MOODS OF SHOES

More often than not we need something to protect our characters' feet. When drawing foot apparel for your characters, don't merely think "formal," "casual" or "boot." Instead, start thinking, "What kind of casual?" "Athletic shoes, sandals or slippers?"

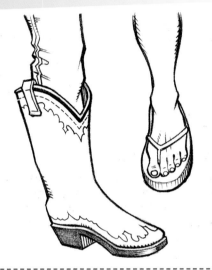
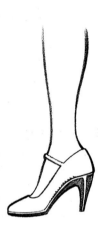
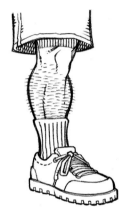
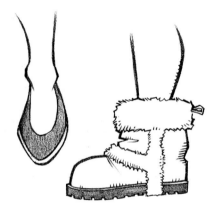

WHERE DO YOU HANG YOURS?

Hats are fun because nowadays they don't have to serve a purpose—they can be worn for pure style. There are many types to choose from, but designing your own can be fun. Of course, there will be situations where certain hats are more appropriate. For instance, a top hat looks better with a tuxedo than a baseball cap!

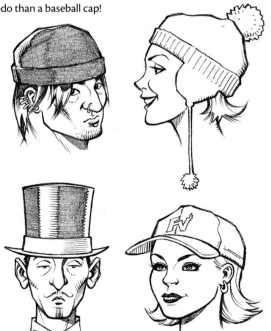

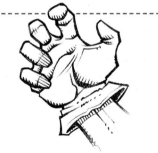
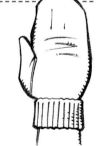

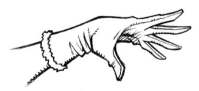

FROM SUPERMODELS TO SKIERS

Gloves serve many purposes, and their design should reflect those purposes. The most common type for non-superhero use is the kind that keeps hands warm; they tend to be thick. Other gloves may protect hands from dirt or grime while others add a touch of elegance.

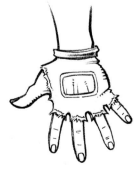

BELTS, GLASSES AND JEWELRY

Even superheroes need something to hold their pants up, and not everybody can have 20/20 vision. Here's some help for drawing those mundane items that get us through the day—or the occasional fight to save the world.

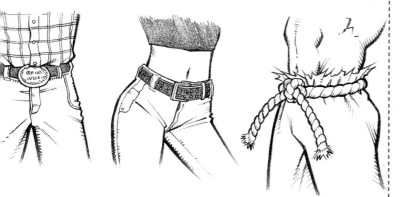

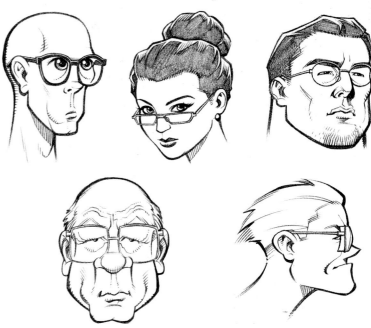

NOT JUST FOR KEEPING YOUR PANTS UP

Some belt designs are suited to females, while others are more male-oriented. Although the belt may come in different lengths, widths and patterns, the buckle is where one can have a little more fun and leeway.

FOUR EYES ARE BETTER THAN TWO

Eyeglasses are a fun accessory. They offer limitless possibilities to enhance the character of a face and establish a person's visual identity. They can tell a little about who's wearing them, too: thick lenses mean poor eyesight, tiny glasses may mean they're used for reading only. An older person wearing thick, horn-rimmed glasses may be stuck in the 1950s.

DECKED OUT

Jewelry—and the amount worn—can say a lot about a character. Typical jewelry includes earrings, necklaces, rings and bracelets; nowadays we also have jewelry for tongues, toes and eyebrows.

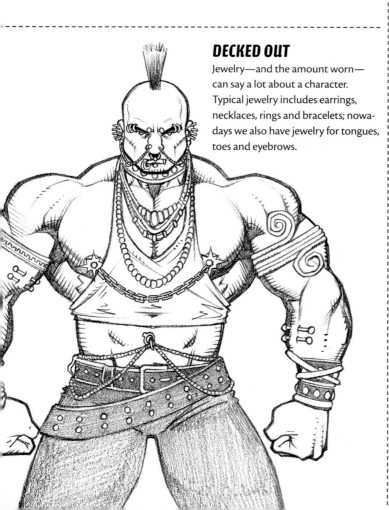

CATCH UP ON THE NEWEST THING!

Besides observing fashions on the street, check clothing catalogs to see what's hip—not just for men and women, but for different age ranges as well.

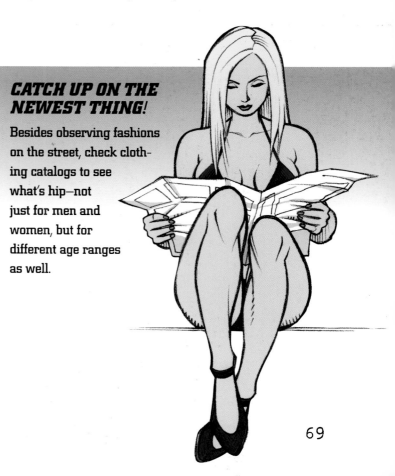

69

SWEATING THE SMALL STUFF

GET THOSE WRINKLES RIGHT!

Sometimes an artist can get bogged down in a certain way of drawing clothing. You can spot this by the generic look of the wrinkles and folds. Their shapes should depend on the underlying body structure, the type and thickness of the fabric and how that fabric is stretched and manipulated. Here are some tips to get you to think more carefully about clothing fabric.

DRESS SHIRT, SWEATER AND SPORT COAT ... NO IRON NEEDED

Different fabrics create different wrinkles. Because certain types of clothing are characterized by certain fabrics, their folds and wrinkles will differ. Notice how the dress shirt, sweater and sports coat in the example at right behave when draped over the same arm position.

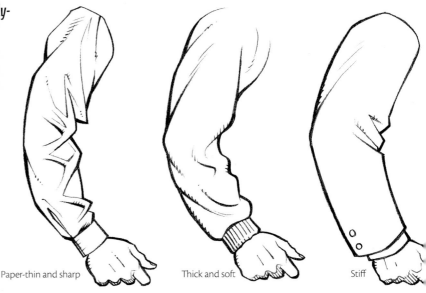

Paper-thin and sharp   Thick and soft   Stiff

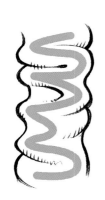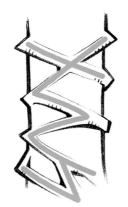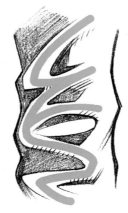

SEE SHAPES AND PATTERNS IN THE FABRIC

When drawing wrinkles along arms and legs, try to see them as shapes that pop out. For instance, some people see them as a roadmap, while others see "tunnels" raised off a surface. How wide are these "canals"? Do they intersect each other? Do they have sharp corners or are they more rounded? Which side of these structures is shaded?

THE BEHAVIOR OF WRINKLES

Wherever there is a bend at a joint (elbows and knees are most common), the fabric will bunch and wrinkle. Wrinkles fan out from this compression and disappear toward the opposite side of the bend, where the fabric is pulled and stretched. On that side, there are no wrinkles.

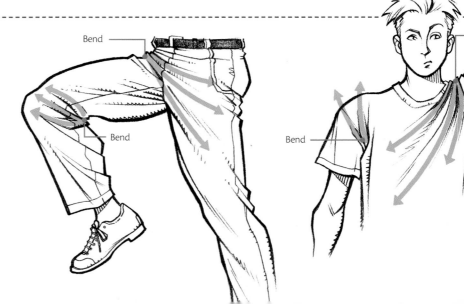

Bend

Bend

Bend

Be

70

GET THOSE BOOBS RIGHT!

A huge peeve of mine is boobs drawn as two separate entities when clothed. GAAH!!! This drives me nuts almost as much as horribly drawn female stomachs! How the hell does the fabric cling so tightly to the underside of the boobs in this example?

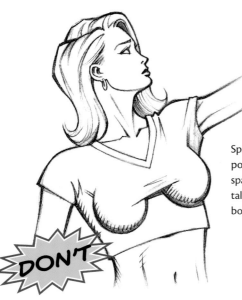

Spare me the "it's supposed to be superhero spandex" excuse. We're talking about big, soft boobs. Draw them right!

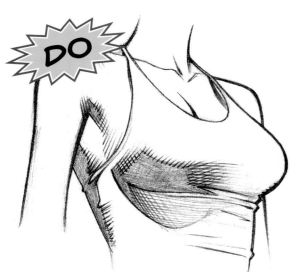

You don't need to stretch the female waist to give the impression of lean sexiness; you don't need to heavily outline clothed breasts to do the same. Pay attention to how fabric drapes and stretches over them.

FORESHORTENED WRINKLES

When you're dealing with foreshortened limbs in clothing, you'll find that wrinkles will oftentimes spiral around the limb like rings. But it isn't just limited to arms and legs; these encircling wrinkles can be found along the trunk and waist of the foreshortened body as well. You can even notice little zig-zag patterns in the wrinkles as well, although they are more tightly compressed due to the foreshortening.

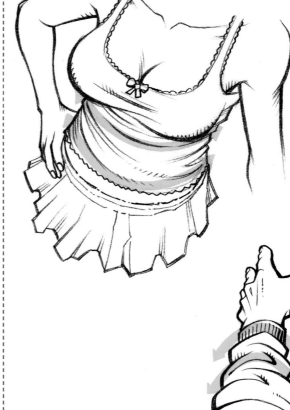

71

PART THREE

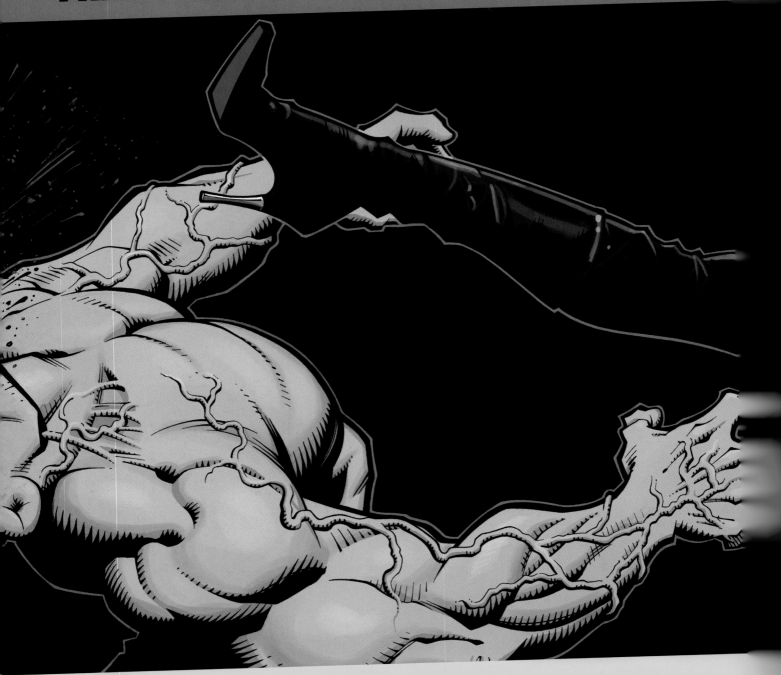

FOR THE
ADVANCED BAD-ASS

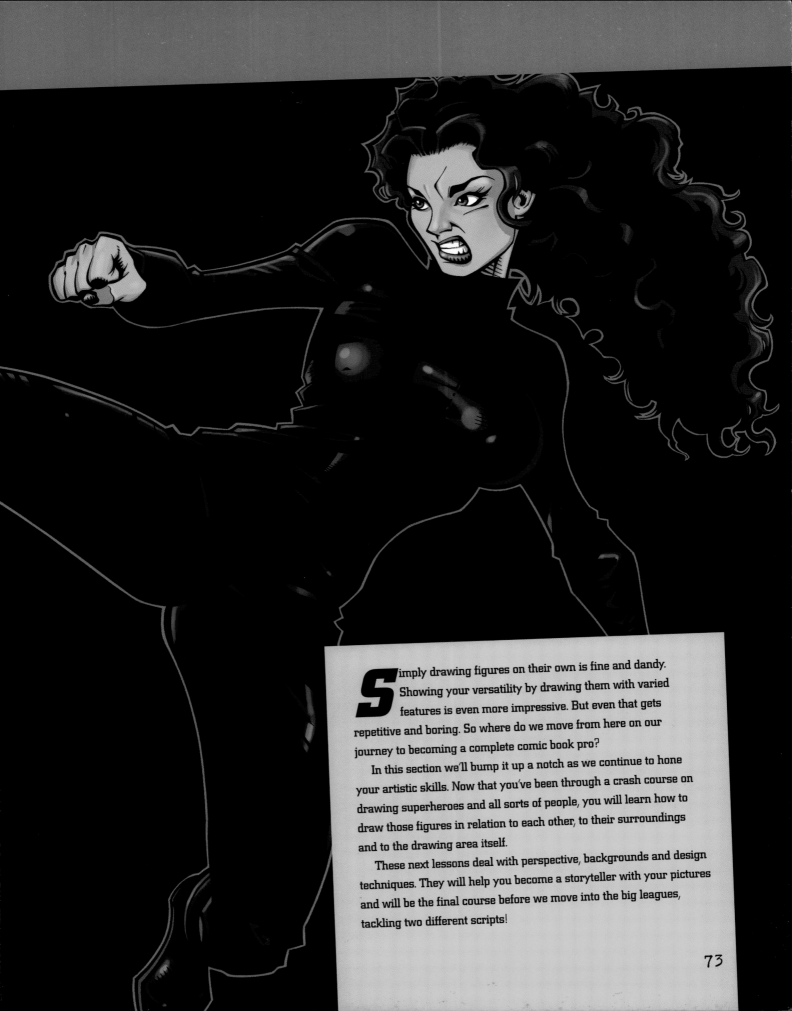

Simply drawing figures on their own is fine and dandy. Showing your versatility by drawing them with varied features is even more impressive. But even that gets repetitive and boring. So where do we move from here on our journey to becoming a complete comic book pro?

In this section we'll bump it up a notch as we continue to hone your artistic skills. Now that you've been through a crash course on drawing superheroes and all sorts of people, you will learn how to draw those figures in relation to each other, to their surroundings and to the drawing area itself.

These next lessons deal with perspective, backgrounds and design techniques. They will help you become a storyteller with your pictures and will be the final course before we move into the big leagues, tackling two different scripts!

ONE-POINT PERSPECTIVE

Welcome to the wonderful world of perspective! It can seem tedious, but take the time to understand these tips and they will definitely bump up your skills a few notches. This is how to make sure everything you draw looks realistic and proportional when things are closer to the viewer than others. There are various types of perspective; we'll look at one-point LINEAR perspective first.

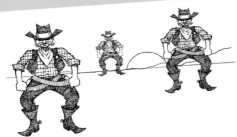

The Horizon Line
The most important aspect of perspective! The horizon line is always the level of your eye. Everything above will cause you to look up, and everything below will cause you to look down. Here are three cowboys at varying distances, but they're not placed properly in relation to the horizon line.

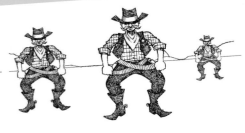

Maintaining the Same Eye Level
Drawing smaller figures is just the beginning. Your eye greets the figures at the same level no matter how far away they are, so the horizon line must run through the same place on every figure (if they're the same height). Here they're in proportion, but in the first example, the farthest cowboy is as tall as a small building!

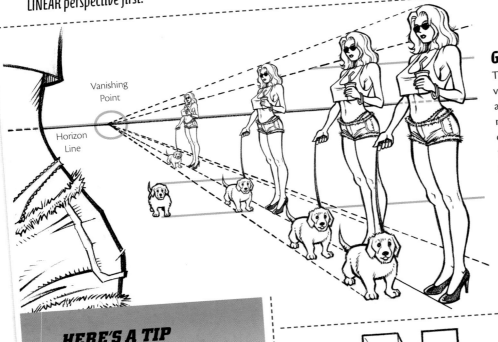

Vanishing Point

Horizon Line

GETTING TECHNICAL

The girl's height gradually decreases toward the vanishing point. If you must draw an object away from your guidelines, visualize where you need to place it along the lines, then shift your object parallel to that position. In the case of the dog, measure how many of its own heights are between it and the horizon line. This number of heights should be consistent no matter what size the dog is.

HERE'S A TIP

You can use one-point perspective to help you more accurately draw your muscles and figures.

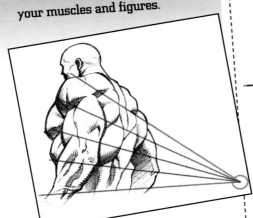

THE VANISHING POINT

In one-point perspective, as lines recede, they converge at a single vanishing point on the horizon line. Lines that don't recede may be parallel or perpendicular to the horizon line. Blocks are easiest to illustrate in perspective, so buildings and cityscapes make easy targets.

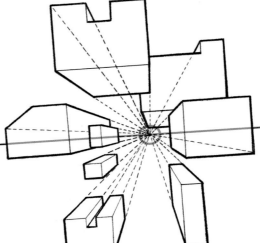

TWO-POINT PERSPECTIVE

Two-point LINEAR perspective is not much more complicated than one-point perspective. Instead of having one vanishing point, we have two of them, spread apart along the horizon line. This form of perspective applies when we look at a block or building whose corner is turned to point straight at us, for example. It adds a bit more dimension to the subject than one-point perspective does.

NOT ONE, BUT TWO VANISHING POINTS!

The two vanishing points are always located to the left and right sides along the horizon line. With the block's corners turned toward us, the tops and bottoms of those blocks are angled left and right, toward each point. Do your best to eyeball how far apart the vanishing points are; the farther apart, the greater the distance in your drawing.

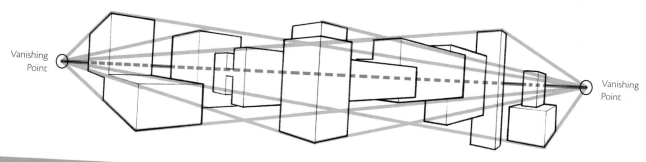

Vanishing Point

Vanishing Point

DEMONSTRATION

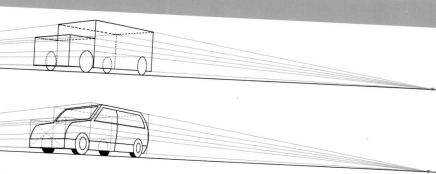

1 ESTABLISH THE HORIZON LINE AND VANISHING POINTS

Construct a boxlike skeletal structure for your subject, in this case an SUV. Visualize the SUV fitting within it. Place the wheels on the far side using the perspective guidelines drawn from the wheels closer to us. All lines recede toward the vanishing points.

2 DRAW A PROPORTIONAL OUTLINE

Using SUV references to get the contours right, draw the simple curves and features in correct proportion within the box. Don't get involved with details; focus on structure and proportion—oh and perspective!

3 MOVING IN

No need for vanishing points while you add more details. See the faint X drawn in the front of the SUV along the box sketch? This helps determine the center of a plane angled in perspective.

4 TIME TO TIGHTEN

Erase the stray, rough lines to clean up our vehicle. It looks realistic, thanks to two-point perspective!

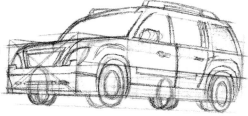

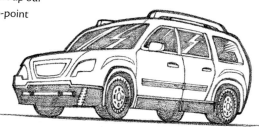

THREE-POINT PERSPECTIVE

One notch up! THREE-POINT PERSPECTIVE is not much different from two-point perspective, except you have a third vanishing point off and away from the horizon line, adding even more dimension to your subjects.

Look at this detail from an upshot city scene (at right). The vanishing points (VPs in the diagrams) are well outside the panel itself. This is perfectly fine; you don't have to keep vanishing points inside the panel unless your panel is extremely big or your buildings are extremely small!

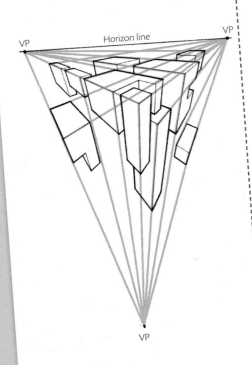

VP · Horizon line · VP

VP

ONE, TWO, THREE!
Place two vanishing points on the horizon line, then add a third well below for a downshot (put the third point above for an upshot). This perspective creates dynamic and cool effects!

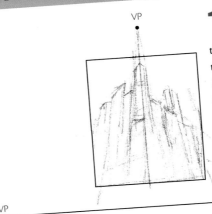

VP

VP · Horizon line · VP

1 DRAW PANEL AND POINTS
Draw the panel and "guess-timate" where the three vanishing points should go. Connect the bottom two to establish the horizon line. Make sure the horizon line is parallel to the bottom edge of the panel.

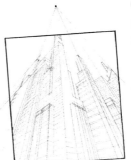

2 STILL ROUGHING FREEHAND
Add more shapes, design and dimension to the initial sketch. Design the buildings any way you want! As you rough, use the vanishing points as guides, drawing toward them.

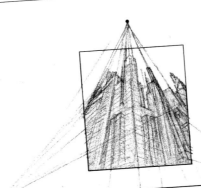

3 RULE PROPER GUIDELINES
I've gotten far enough. These formal guidelines will help finish the drawing, and provide checkpoints for a freehand rough. Don't freehand too deeply, so you can erase parts that are misaligned.

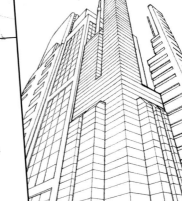

4 CAREFULLY CHOOSE LINES
Ignore the ones you don't need! I generally start with the outlines of each building (working broadly), then work my way into details such as ledges, windows and so forth. A dynamic use of perspective, indeed!

CURVILINEAR PERSPECTIVE

CURVILINEAR PERSPECTIVE (sometimes called four- or five-point perspective) is downright wonky and can make you dizzy in high doses! It's like looking through a wide-angle lens; the picture is extremely distorted and lines you know to be straight are curved, as if encircling a globe. Its purpose is to show a wide panoramic scene. It's a unique way of drawing that does, however, involve a little mental strain.

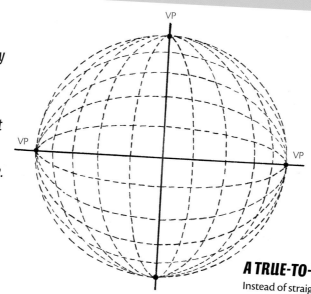

A TRUE-TO-LIFE PORTRAYAL

Instead of straight lines, your eye sees lines curving toward the vanishing points. Line compression and distortion is increased as you move away from the center (your vantage point), and objects appear squeezed together near the vanishing points. Visualize a gridded globe.

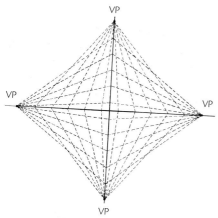

FOUR-POINT PERSPECTIVE

The idea is to be able to see all of a scene's receding sides in a single shot. The fourth point is on the opposite side of the horizon line from the third. We now have four: left, right, above and below, all equally spaced. Your own vantage point, right in the center, is considered the fifth point. This example doesn't show that since it's composed of straight lines, but your eye doesn't portray panoramic scenes this way.

DEMONSTRATION

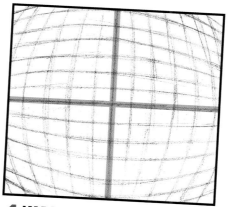

1 IMAGINE A CIRCULAR GRID

In comic books, if you were to draw a smaller scene with a little curvilinear distortion, you wouldn't need to rule an entire circular grid. Sometimes you can get your point across convincingly by "eyeballing" where the curved lines should go, and how curved they should be. Here is a rough of a limited curvilinear scene. Just make sure the bow of the lines is a little more noticeable on all four sides as you move away from the center.

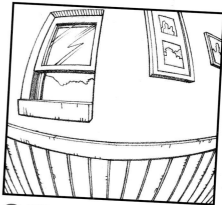

2 MIND-BENDING PERSPECTIVE

You can see how the simple concept of the previous step can be used to create a unique view of this wall with a window. In the end, distortion is distortion, and that means that you can even bend the rules (ha-ha) to your liking, as long as they seem to converge toward vanishing points.

ADDING SPICE TO YOUR CITY

It wasn't until I met big-shot artist Doug Mahnke at age fifteen that I realized backgrounds not only add so much to a story, but that without them, I wouldn't have a shot in comics! Backgrounds give your characters a place to be. Trying to get away with no backgrounds will only expose you as a hack.

Most backgrounds rely on perspective, but not all backgrounds are the same. The trick to drawing a convincing and interesting city is to notice the little things. Sure, it's easy to draw rectangular blocks for buildings, but what about their surfaces? What about windows? Streets? What makes one structure or road different from another?

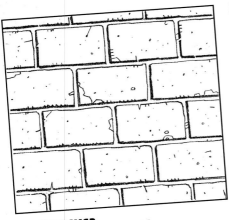

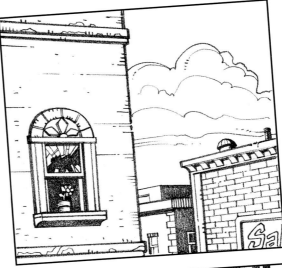

AVOID THE PLAIN OLD EDGES AND CORNERS

How about making an interesting ledge? Not just for the tops, but for the building's middle and the windows as well. Heck, break the windows if you want!

GOT BRICKS?

Make the lines imperfect and add dots and dashes for texture and character.

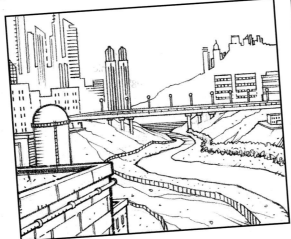

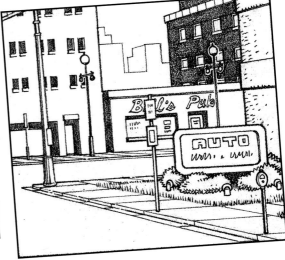

NOT EVERYTHING IS FLAT

Creating uneven surfaces and building heights can add that special something to your city scene.

KEEP IT BUSY!

Signs and lights are a great way to decorate your streets. They can be of different heights and designs as well.

ENVIRONMENTAL SCENES

Occasionally, you may have to draw backgrounds that deal with nature. This may seem easier in that you don't need to rule any grids, but you'll still have to draw natural-looking things to pull it off. Use organic, freehand lines in place of stiff, mechanical ones.

They should be irregular, soft and curvy (except for things like jagged rocks). Texture is key in nature and will help to distinguish objects from one another.

A PLETHORA OF LINES

Leaves and foliage offer quite a bit of line variety and therefore, different ways of rendering them.

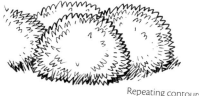

Repeating contours within the form

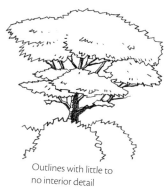

Outlines with little to no interior detail

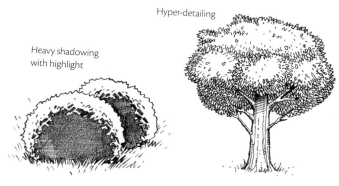

Heavy shadowing with highlight

Hyper-detailing

DON'T Would you believe that these are blades of grass? They look like a wacky bar code!

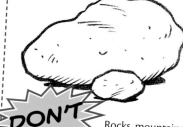

DON'T Rocks, mountains and other hard textures are an exception to the soft, organic lines rule. This rock looks like pudding!

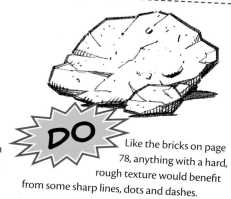

DO Like the bricks on page 78, anything with a hard, rough texture would benefit from some sharp lines, dots and dashes.

DO Grass is achieved with a combination of quick, upside-down *V* strokes and single lines. The longer your blades, the more they should curve. Make them smaller and fainter as they recede into the background.

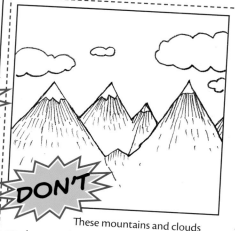

DON'T These mountains and clouds are almost as despicable as the "bar code" grass—typical and template-like.

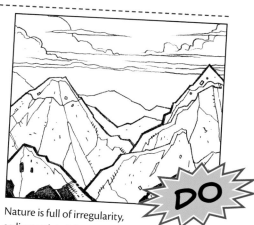

DO Nature is full of irregularity, so line variety is key to realistic drawing. The softness of the clouds is a wonderful contrast to the hard, jagged-ness of the mountains.

79

FUTURISTIC/SPACE SCENES

Futuristic scenes are fun because they rely solely on your imagination (unless you own a time machine). Still, there are some loose guidelines to follow in portraying a convincing science-fiction scene. Like city scenes, futuristic scenes tend to be less organic and more mechanical. Pretty trees and flowers are out! This is not to say you can't have sleek curves, however.

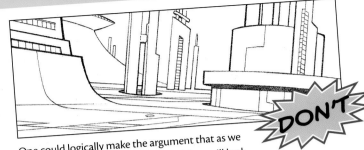

One could logically make the argument that as we get more technologically advanced, things will look sleeker and simpler. Fair enough, but look how ridiculously boring this is! This is the one area where the "less is more" rule is thrown out.

DEMONSTRATION

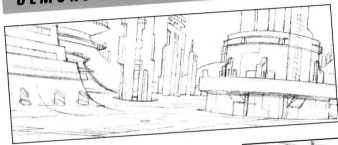

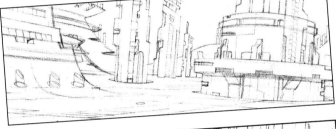

1 START WITH A BASE
We'll take that boring background and jazz it up a bit. Add smaller geometric structures and shapes onto the existing shapes. Remember to use perspective (now that you know how!) where it can apply.

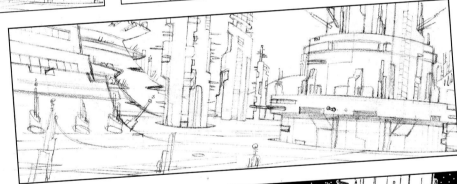

2 CARVE GAPS, NOOKS AND CRANNIES
You can already see a lot of character develop in your scene. Plan your shadows to show depth and dimension.

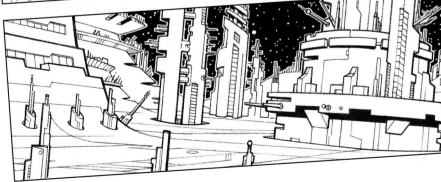

3 JUST ADD THINGS!
A cool trick is to add a lot of cylindrical projections and antenna-like things poking out here and there. More is better!

4 VOILÀ!
Finishing touches like thin, irregular texture lines along surfaces and series of little squares or boxes will complete your scene. As for the perspective tutorials, choose your lines and ignore rough understructures. Scatter stars around for effect!

ATMOSPHERIC PERSPECTIVE

Like linear perspective, ATMOSPHERIC PERSPECTIVE helps to establish the position of objects within space. However, atmospheric perspective doesn't deal with grids and technical measuring. Instead, it focuses on how an object's appearance changes as it recedes into the distance. We'll see blurriness, loss of detail, loss of contrast and blueness (if we're dealing with color) in very distant objects. This occurs because the air isn't completely transparent and its effects are magnified as we move farther away—hence the term ATMOSPHERIC perspective. It's a very powerful technique for creating depth in your scenes.

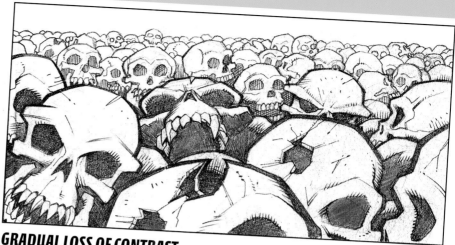

GRADUAL LOSS OF CONTRAST

The most basic way of showing distance is thicker lines in the foreground and progressively thinner lines going back. Nearby objects show a healthy amount of contrast. As objects recede, light and dark start to "gray out." If your object is black, simulate grays by crosshatching. For extreme distances, avoid blacks altogether.

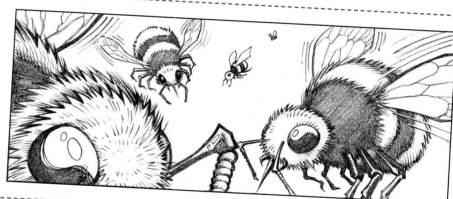

GRADUAL LOSS OF DETAIL

Instead of drawing all the details even smaller in receding objects, try easing off. The atmosphere reduces the amount of detail we can see in distant objects. Save your eyes the strain!

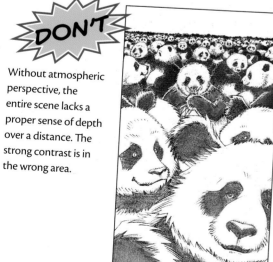

Without atmospheric perspective, the entire scene lacks a proper sense of depth over a distance. The strong contrast is in the wrong area.

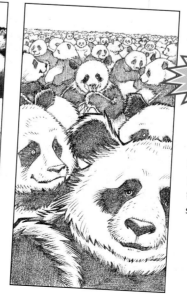

Depth is achieved through the diminishing clarity of the bears in the distance. This perfectly illustrates the power of atmospheric perspective.

COMPOSITION PRINCIPLES

COMPOSITION is basically the arrangement of objects and elements in a drawing. Although you can arrange them any way you want, some arrangements will be more effective than others.

Now that you've been through a crash course on how to draw various elements, we'll discuss how to organize them on your blank paper. It seems simple enough: just draw what you want, where you want it, right? True, it can be that simple. But I'm about to put you through a crash course in composition so you can learn how to get others to see what you want them to see in your art.

When you look at others' artwork, what gets your attention first? What little things do you notice? What guides your eye to the most interesting part? Developing you own composition skills will aid you tremendously in your quest to become a big-time professional comic artist.

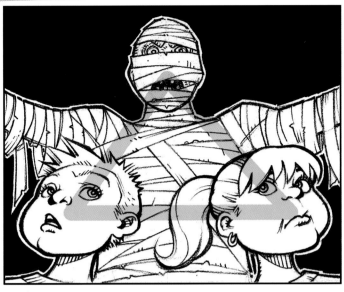

TRIANGULAR COMPOSITION

This is a classic tool for those new to the concept of composing art. Triangular composition involves distributing your elements around the three points of an imaginary triangle on your drawing space. This simple concept is effective because the triangle is a dynamic yet stable shape that conveys unity. It also helps to move the eye around the composition.

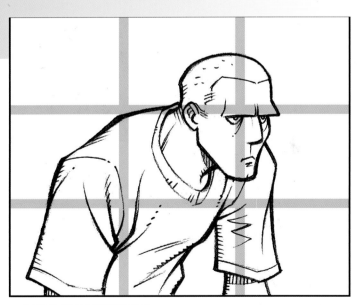

THE RULE OF THIRDS

Here's another old trick used by artists and photographers. It involves dividing your space vertically and horizontally into thirds, kind of like a tic-tac-toe grid. Place your center of interest at one of the imaginary intersections created by the dividing lines. By moving your focal point slightly off center this way, you create a more interesting composition. More so than you would by placing your subject smack-dab in the middle.

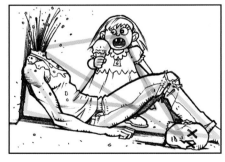

USE A VARIETY OF TRIANGLES

You don't always have to use a perfect triangle that covers your entire space. Be creative and use asymmetrical triangles; in fact, try combining and using multiple triangle shapes in your drawings.

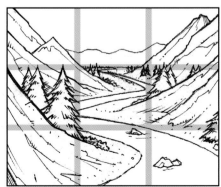

COMPOSING WITH PERSPECTIVE

Placing the horizon line along one of the dividing lines is an effective way to compose a scene.

BALANCE

BALANCE is achieved by evenly distributing the "weight" of the elements in a scene. Depending on how you decide to distribute them, you can emphasize certain parts of the composition (more on this later). First, though, let's look at different types of balance.

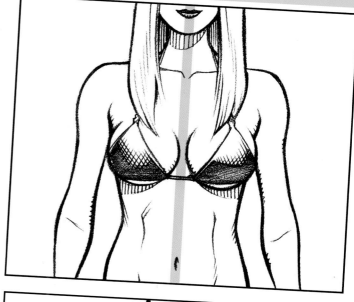

SYMMETRY

When a composition is symmetrical both the left and right sides (or the top and bottom, depending) more or less mirror each other. (Tay's boobs are a fine example.) Even if elements on either side aren't exactly the same, symmetrical balance can be achieved if they have similar characteristics and weight.

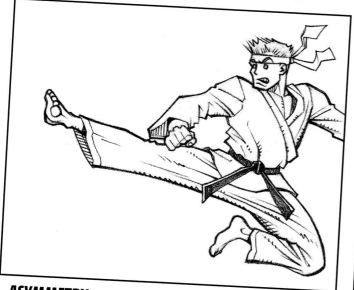

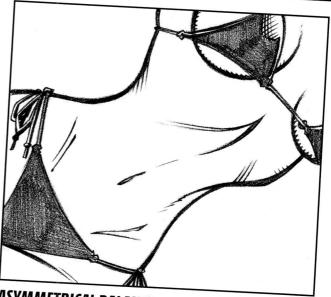

ASYMMETRY

Asymmetrical compositions have very different elements on the left and right sides (or the top and bottom) of the drawing area.

ASYMMETRICAL BALANCE

Balance can be achieved in an asymmetrical composition by carefully placing elements to add weight where you need it. In this case, the ends of an hourglass-like shape have roughly equal weight. (Thanks again, Tay!)

EMPHASIS, CONTRAST AND UNITY

Deciding on an AREA OF EMPHASIS or a FOCAL POINT for your work is fairly easy because you usually know where you want the viewer to look first. The trick is deciding HOW to draw the eye to that center of interest. Many artists do this by placing their main subjects right in the middle of the panel, but that type of composition gets boring fast. Use the rule of thirds to locate your focal point in a more pleasing position, then emphasize it with some type of CONTRAST. Contrast can be achieved in a variety of ways.

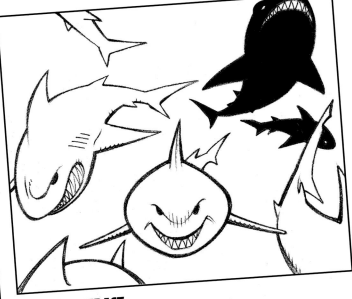

VALUE CONTRAST

Value refers to the darkness or lightness of an object. When we went over atmospheric perspective (page 81), we saw that value contrasts can add a sense of depth to an image. You can also use value contrasts to emphasize a portion of a scene, as illustrated here.

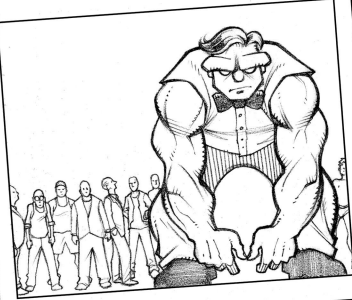

SIZE CONTRAST

Size is an easy way to show your emphasis. The bigger the subject in relation to other elements, the more attention it draws.

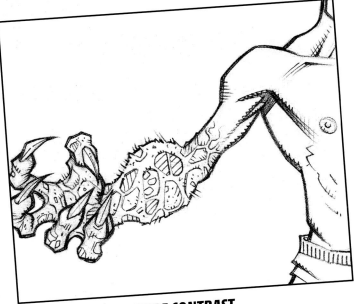

PATTERNS AND TEXTURE CONTRAST

Contrasts in patterns and textures can direct your attention as well.

UNITY AND VARIETY

UNITY means creating harmony in the entire composition. Your picture may be composed of many diverse elements, but how can you pull them together to achieve a harmonious effect? Use repetition to unify your composition while maintaining an interesting variety of forms.

PATTERN REPETITION

Repeating patterns throughout the picture can pull an entire scene together. Here, areas that have been crosshatched in the same direction help to unify different elements in the drawing.

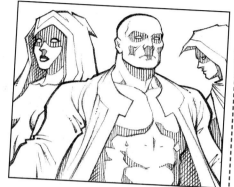

TEXTURE REPETITION

Repeated textures also help to unify a panel with multiple objects.

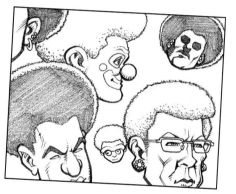

SHAPE REPETITION

Similar shapes placed throughout your drawing can add harmony to an otherwise cluttered panel.

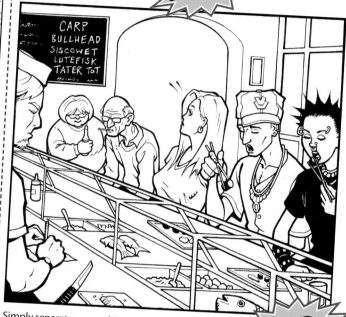

Overlapping forms is OK, but avoid butting the outline of one form right against another. Outlines that accidentally connect are called tangents, and tangents are very confusing to the eye because they make it difficult to distinguish one form from another.

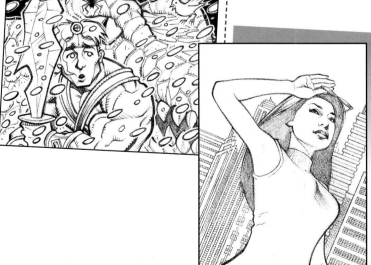

Simply separate your subjects, or make sure there is a clear intersection of lines to avoid confusion.

DIAGONAL SCENES

Turning the whole scene at a slight diagonal will do wonders to create more dynamism and make your drawing pop! Diagonals have a wonderful way of creating a sense of movement even when there is technically no movement.

STYLE VS. POOR DRAWING

OH, THAT'S JUST MY STYLE

What is an artist's style? How does it work with drawing ability? Learning how things are put together and how to draw them with relative accuracy according to certain principles is the technical side of art. This includes learning anatomy, perspective, basic construction, proportions, and principles of light and shadow. "But there are no rules in art," you say. Wow, what a popular comment! Technically it's true, but in the field of competitive illustration, certain basic drawing skills ("rules") must reach a level of proficiency before one can become a pro. I think a more accurate statement would be: "But there are no rules to style."

Then what is style? Style is how you decide to demonstrate and apply your technical skills (assuming that you've learned them!). Style is what distinguishes one artist's work from another's. When an artist develops and refines a personal style and uses it consistently, that style will become identifiable throughout the artist's work. Styles can range from very weird to very slick. Flashy, detailed styles tend to look cooler to kids because they grab their attention.

You can probably guess that I would stress learning to draw correctly before adding your own "twist." I always say that you have to walk before you can run; if you have substance, any way you decide to interpret that substance will look OK. Style with no substance will make drawings that look "off" and half-assed. I get ticked off when I hear an artist respond to a critique with an answer like, "Oh, that's just my style; that's part of exaggeration in comics." Using style to defend a lack of technical proficiency is a big no-no and a poor excuse in my book.

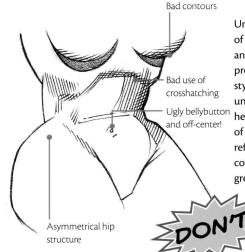

Bad contours

Bad use of crosshatching

Ugly bellybutton and off-center!

Asymmetrical hip structure

DON'T

Understanding principles of structural foundation and proportion must precede development of style. Unfortunately, that understanding is lacking here, and no amount of flashy lines—often referred to as "style"—can cover up this mess. (I greatly enjoy ragging on poorly drawn stomachs and women, as you well know by now.)

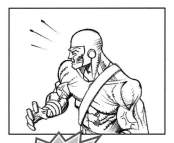 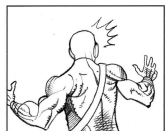

DON'T

Consistency is another clue to whether the artist knows what he or she is doing. In this example, the upper body details are drawn inconsistently in two separate panels. This is an error, not a style issue.

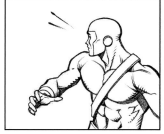 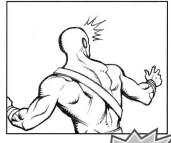

Obviously, you want to stay consistent to maintain continuity and believability.

DO

C'MON!

You wouldn't want to read a whole comic drawn like this, would ya?

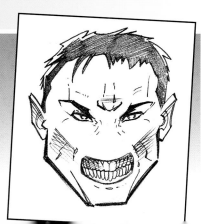

86

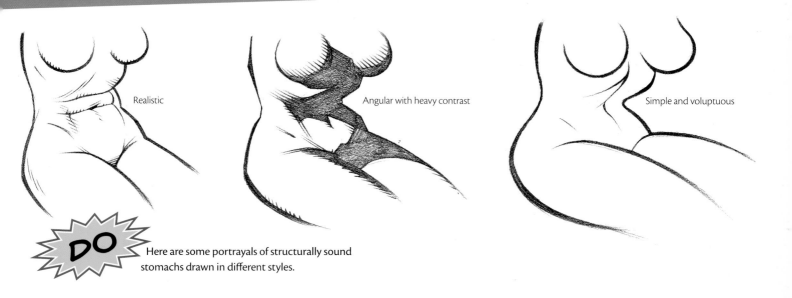

Realistic

Angular with heavy contrast

Simple and voluptuous

DO Here are some portrayals of structurally sound stomachs drawn in different styles.

THE MOST REMARKABLE MACHINE

Remember the anatomy lessons in this book? The human body works and moves the way it does because it's put together in a certain way. It truly is the most remarkable machine ever! And like all machines, if it's not assembled correctly, it won't work. Look at this incorrectly drawn shoulder (the deltoid overlaps the collarbone).

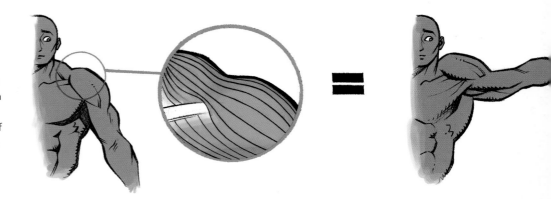

IT'S NOT STYLE, IT'S JUST BAD

Let's say that you were to use "comic book exaggeration" as a stylistic excuse for your anatomical errors. By that theory, why not draw eyes off center and the height of the nose above the eyes every now and then? Let's see how far you get with this "style"! While we're at it, let's hire a first-grader to draw our favorite monthly comics and chalk it up to "style" as well!

Obviously, what is said here goes for other technical drawing errors—especially in perspective, where I feel the "rules" are much more rigid than in figure drawing. Bodies vary greatly in form, so naturally, some variation in their proportions is acceptable.

It certainly helps to follow trends in style in order keep up to date with what's cool; otherwise you'll run the risk of being labeled "old-school." But if you strive for a trendy look, you risk being labeled as a copycat artist. It's a fine line to walk.

Sometimes artists worry too much about style. My best advice is to learn to draw things well, and the style will come naturally. You'll probably even develop a unique look faster than someone who drives him- or herself nuts trying to figure out a unique and cool style before learning how to draw. I should know—I used to be one of those kids.

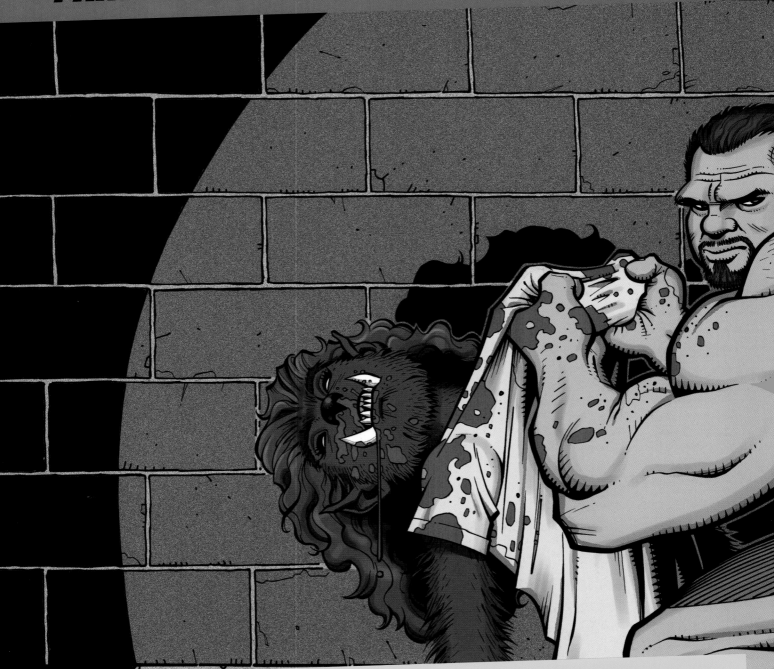

PART FOUR

YOUR OWN KICK-ASS COMICS

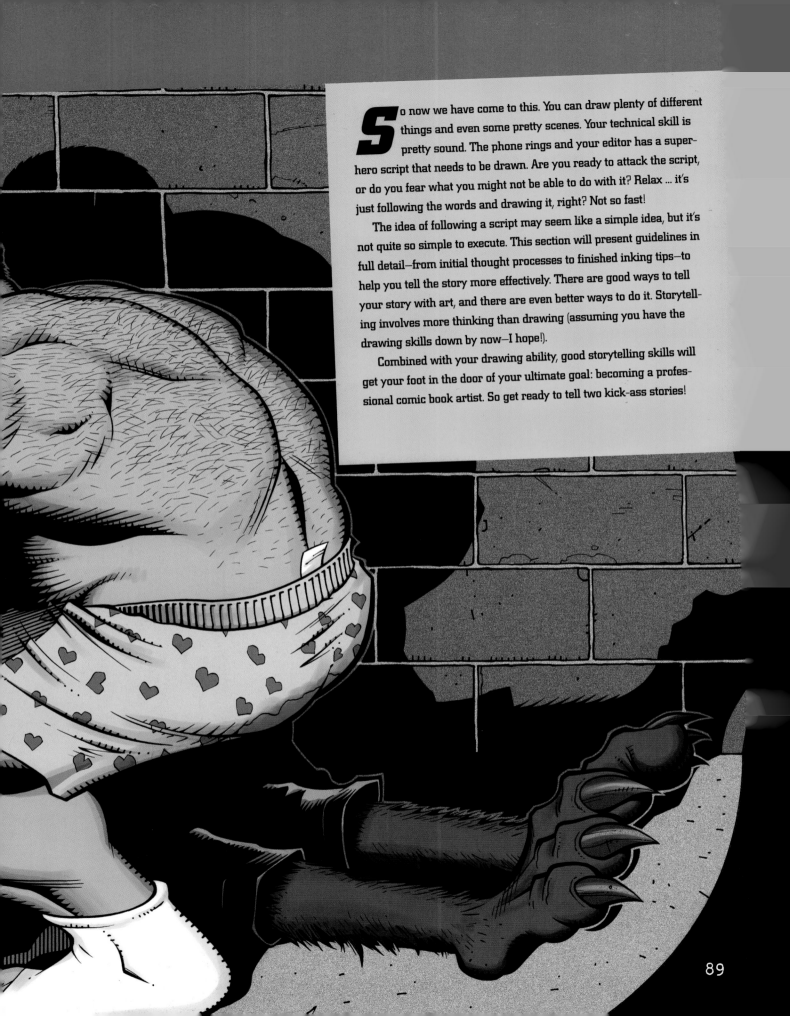

So now we have come to this. You can draw plenty of different things and even some pretty scenes. Your technical skill is pretty sound. The phone rings and your editor has a super-hero script that needs to be drawn. Are you ready to attack the script, or do you fear what you might not be able to do with it? Relax ... it's just following the words and drawing it, right? Not so fast!

The idea of following a script may seem like a simple idea, but it's not quite so simple to execute. This section will present guidelines in full detail—from initial thought processes to finished inking tips—to help you tell the story more effectively. There are good ways to tell your story with art, and there are even better ways to do it. Storytelling involves more thinking than drawing (assuming you have the drawing skills down by now—I hope!).

Combined with your drawing ability, good storytelling skills will get your foot in the door of your ultimate goal: becoming a professional comic book artist. So get ready to tell two kick-ass stories!

REVIEWING THE SCRIPT

REI: TEENAGE SAMURAI

Here we'll work with a script aimed at the typical superhero fantasy audience. It's got a combination of cool characters, dialogue and action scenes—the perfect recipe for a comic book page!

OUR PROTAGANIST

Our main character will be a girl named Rei, created by artist-writer extraordinaire Keith Champagne and myself. Rei is a teenage samurai who is about to do battle with a mythical Japanese creature. In order to begin, we have to look at the script and prepare our imagination.

SKILLS THAT PAY THE UM, UH ... BILLS!

Demonstrating these storytelling skills will greatly benefit your portfolio and help you on your quest to comic book stardom.

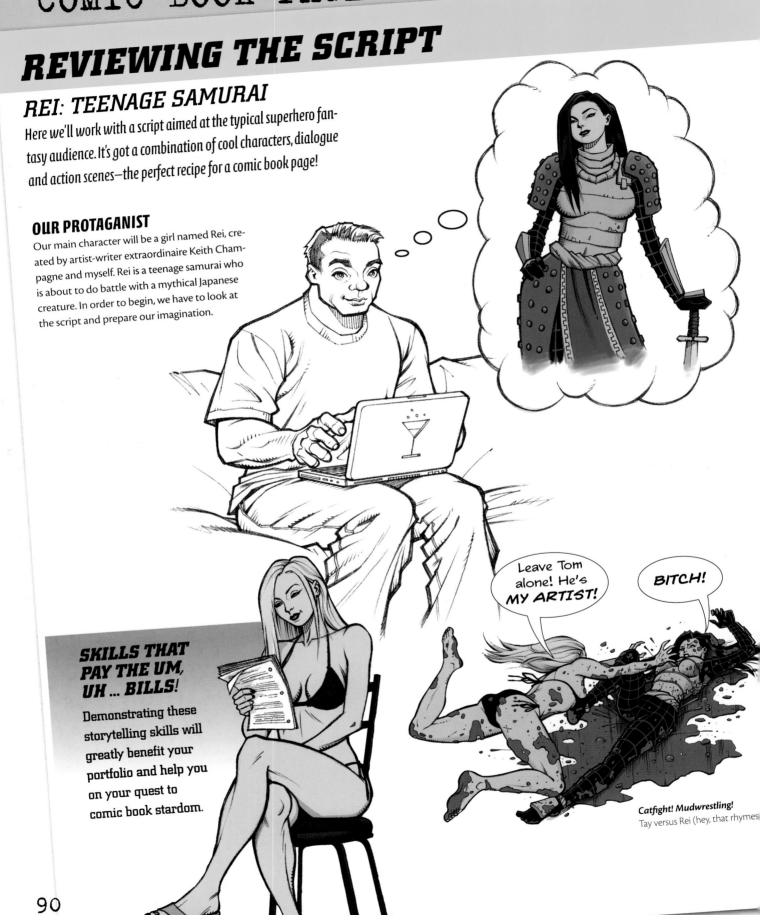

Leave Tom alone! He's MY ARTIST!

BITCH!

Catfight! Mudwrestling!
Tay versus Rei (hey, that rhymes

READING THE SCRIPT

Keith's script is a five-panel page. You'll notice that right away he provides an Internet reference for our dragon. If the writer is good (and kind enough!), he will provide any necessary references that his artist may need in order to draw things accurately. In this case, Keith provided links to sites online that show me examples of our dragon and the samurai armor that Rei is supposed to wear. It's not necessary to be a slave to photo references (especially in the case of our mythical dragon, where there can be several interpretations). Feel free to use your artistic license to play with the visuals as long as you show the basic gist of things.

PAY ATTENTION TO THE DIALOGUE

Try to hear what the characters are saying when you draw poses and expressions. It will help you to draw a more honest and thoughtful scene.

Feel free to communicate with your writer (if you choose to work with scripts other than your own) if you have any questions. After all, you're a team, and the project is your baby. And everyone wants to be proud of their baby!

KEITH'S SCRIPT: "THE BUTTERFLY SAMURAI"

PANEL ONE
(Tom, for a history lesson and reference on the dragon: http://en.wikipedia.org/wiki/Japanese_dragon and http://en.wikipedia.org/wiki/Orochi.)

In the depths of the cavernous dragon's nest far below Mount Fuji, the fearsome dragon, Yamato No Orochi, rises up, finally reunited with its heart. Seven of its eight heads flex, whirling and roaring, rejoicing in the sensation of being reborn after seven hundred years of death. Its eighth head ...

Glares down at Rei, its eyes glowing with power and hatred. Flame drips from its mouth like venom, fiery drops splashing the ground at her feet.

Rei's back is to the reader. She's standing defiantly in front of Yamato No Orochi and raises her grandfather's katana, clutched firmly in both hands, toward the great beast. She's dressed in traditional samurai garb, sans the helmet. Her hair is blowing in the sulfuric breath of the dragon.
(For a reference on Samurai armor: http://www.japanese-armor.com/japanese-armor.shtml.)

1- YAMATO NO ORICHI: Your hands tremble, little butterfly.

2- YAMATO NO ORICHI: Your fear smells DELICIOUS ...

PANEL TWO
Close on Yamato No Orichi. The beast is smiling, pure evil.

3- YAMATO NO ORICHI: ... And it has been far too long since I've FEASTED.

PANEL THREE
Angle on Rei. Her face is slightly charred from the dragon's hot breath, her cheeks lightly dusted with soot. She does look scared, although she's trying hard not to show it. Her butterfly totem is fluttering to a landing on her shoulder.

4- REI: I ... I ... I ...

PANEL FOUR
Rei finds her courage, fortified by the sudden appearance of her butterfly totem. Her eyes narrow angrily, ready for battle.

5- REI: Only a fool rejects fear, beast.

6- REI: My GRANDFATHER taught me better.

PANEL FIVE
Rei leaps toward Yamato No Orichi, attacking with her sword.

7- REI: Come.

8- REI: See what I've learned.

91

THUMBNAIL LAYOUTS

Before you can begin drawing your page, you have to decide how you want your page to be laid out. Do this by sketching little doodles called thumbnails. These thumbnails can be a couple of inches high and are an effective way to quickly get your ideas on paper. Doing several thumbnail sketches allows you to keep the best elements and discard the worst.

Some layouts get your point across better than others. You must consider readability, design, impact (focus) panels, character placement and poses, contrast and camera angles.

Here I've created several thumbnail layouts of Keith's script to see which one works best. You may like only certain parts of a thumbnail while prefering parts of another, so don't be afraid to mix and match panels to get the best effect.

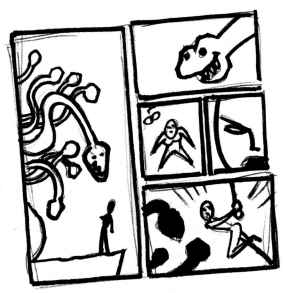

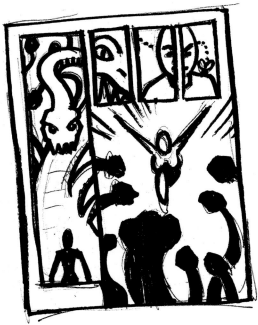

1 HERE WE GO!

For my first attempt, I wanted a dramatic opening: a panel fit for an introduction, showing both the dragon and Rei. But I didn't know whether I wanted the first or the last panel to be the emphatic, big one. It's typical to make the last action panel the biggest, but it could be a setup for a *huge* panel lurking on the next page.

The tall opening panel, showing the dragon and Rei from the side, is not pulled back as far as a typical establishing shot of, say, a city scene, but it's enough to show them both interacting. The reader's natural flow of vision is from left to right and top to bottom, so the rest of the panels are to the right of this big one. In the second panel, the angle of the dragon's head helps direct the reader to the third panel. Notice how simple and sloppy the layout is. Thumbnails are just for you; they're not meant to be masterpieces.

2 ANOTHER STAB

Keeping the long, vertical panel format, I narrowed it a bit to make more room for a bigger final panel. I moved the camera angle a bit to experiment with a different vantage point (in this case, right behind Rei). Rei is in silhouette because I wanted to showcase the monster more. It's not like we're seeing her from the front anyway.

I arranged the three dialogue panels together in one row at the top of the right half of the page, providing more space for a bigger final panel. Panels three and four demonstrate a trick you see every now and then: one scene or subject is split into two separate panels. Each of those panels is drawn slightly differently to show the passage of time. In this case, Rei's butterfly buzzes behind her and lands on her shoulder. The last panel is significantly bigger than its counterpart in the first thumbnail. It's a typical jumping-right-at-you pose with action lines coming in from the border—a little cliché

3 SIMPLIFYING

This straightforward orientation leads your eye from left to right, and then down. And let's face it, there's no way the talking-head panels are going to be bigger than the first or last panel. When there is dialogue between two subjects, I like to keep their heads turned toward each other, even if they are in separate panels, to give a better impression of their interaction. Also, when I know that a talking head is in a panel butted up to either the left or right side of the page, I like to turn the head to face inward; otherwise it might seem that Rei is talking to someone off the page. The last panel is big, with potential to show some great foreshortening (page 28) from this angle.

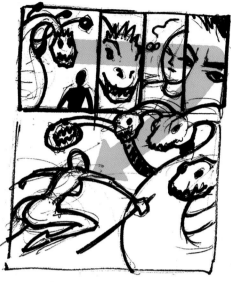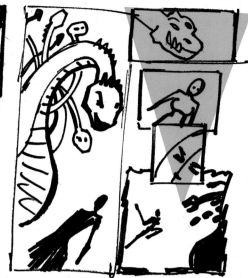

4 GETTING DOWN TO THE WIRE

Can you tell that I like the vertical opening panel? I will carry it over somehow into the final version. This time I tilted the opening scene a bit to make it more interesting. On the right half of the page, I have panels two through four stacked and diminishing in size leading to the final panel. It forms a kind of arrow that points the eye downward, but at the same time, it's a little cheesy-looking. Because the last panel is a quiet silhouette, heightening the anticipation of the action to follow on the next page, the gestures of Rei and the dragon are of utmost importance.

5 FINALLY!

This one's got the best elements from the previous panels "frankensteined" into one. I've decided to give the first and last panels fairly equal weight and importance, with the in-between panels being quieter. No surprise, I kept the vertical first panel, but this time it's more of an upward view of the dragon, giving us a sense of its impressive size as it leers down upon us (and Rei). The next three panels are like those in attempt two—small and across the top, leaving plenty of room for the last panel. Panel two is self-explanatory, a closeup of a dragon head talking. The third and fourth panels are of Rei. First, her body is shown so we can see what she and her outfit look like. Then we get a dramatic closeup of her meanie eyes. Both of her panels are angled in the same direction to indicate that the same character is talking, and the diagonal orientation directs the eye down to the last panel.

Adding jagged borders for emphasis, I went with the dynamic angle of attempt four for this last scene. I lowered the vantage point and foreshortened Rei a bit more to push the dynamics. Plus, another butt shot never hurts! This view will show Rei in action and the dragon in full glory.

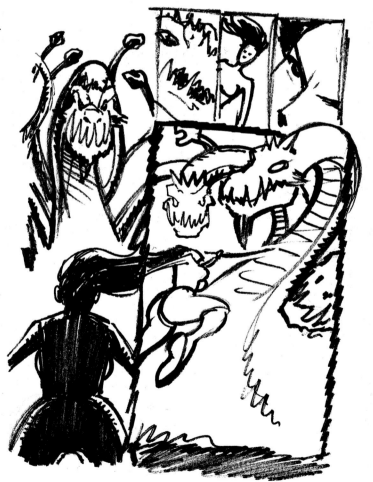

ROUGHING OUT THE PAGE

Now I can start to draw the page using the "winning" thumbnail. When referring to the thumbnail rough, I'll loosely sketch what I see in the thumbs onto the full-size, 11" × 17" (28cm × 43cm) bristol board. Some artists use a projector to enlarge their thumbnails onto a full-size board, or make enlargements with a photocopier, usually because they've drawn tight thumbnail sketches and don't feel the need to redraw them from scratch. I am much too lazy to set up or even get to a machine to make an enlargement, and since my thumbs are so sloppy anyway, it's no big deal for me to re-rough straight onto the board.

USE THE ENTIRE PAGE

Draw panel one as if it were going to cover the entire page. It's important not to skip this process. Drawing only what's visible within the panel's frame may result in misalignment. Notice that the necks are S-shapes galore!

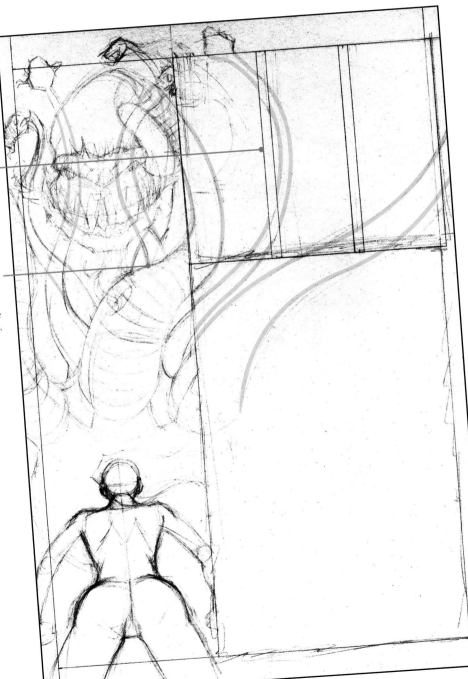

The first thing I do is rule in my panels with a T-square so I know where each panel will be located and how much space I have to work with. The gutters between panels two, three and four have a width of ¼-inch (6 mm).

The borderless opening panel has to be drawn across the page so that the dragon necks can continue behind the other panels. Glimpses of the necks will be visible in the gutters between panels.

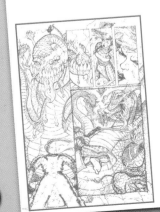

PANEL 1: ADD DETAIL TO THE BASIC FORMS

Let's look more closely at the first panel itself. We've laid in the basic shapes first and will add more complex elements on top. Remember the lesson about drawing in the figure before you put clothing on top? No exception here. Rei's figure was already roughed in, so now we can add all her gear. Because the samurai outfit is rather complex, take plenty of time to figure it out—unless you're an expert at costume design.

The upshot view lets us see that the fiery drool is falling downward toward us. It follows the perspective guidelines (in red).

Dragon necks are essentially long tubes. Visualize coils around them to help you draw the scales on their undersides. These will help show dimension and foreshortening.

Notice the guidelines throughout Rei's arms, legs and body as we are treated to an upshot angle of her figure. The costume is accurately roughed in over her body.

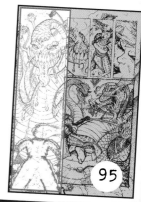

ROUGHING OUT PANELS 2, 3 AND 4

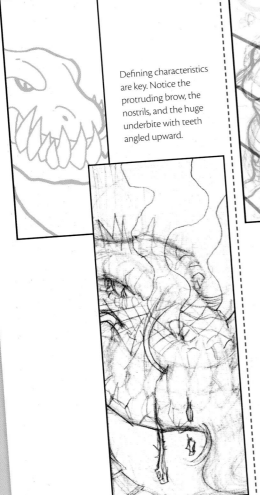

Defining characteristics are key. Notice the protruding brow, the nostrils, and the huge underbite with teeth angled upward.

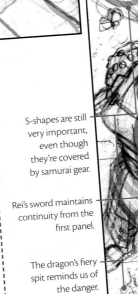

The angle of her eyebrows reveals hesitant anger.

S-shapes are still very important, even though they're covered by samurai gear.

Rei's sword maintains continuity from the first panel.

The dragon's fiery spit reminds us of the danger.

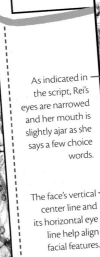

As indicated in the script, Rei's eyes are narrowed and her mouth is slightly ajar as she says a few choice words.

The face's vertical center line and its horizontal eye line help align facial features.

PANEL 2: THE MAIN DRAGONHEAD

Starting with a simple line drawing of the head, I've added more features such as the spikes on top, the forked tongue curling between the teeth, smoke coming out of the nostrils and fiery drool. I've also added a rough, irregular "grid" as a guide for scales to be finished later.

PANEL 3: REI GAZES NERVOUSLY

Start with the basic shapes and curved contours to accurately place the armor.

Take note of the lines that are normally parallel to the ground: the shoulders, breasts, hip bones, knees and feet. From this angle, those levels become diagonals, converging to a far off vanishing point. Use perspective to give your figure credibility in unusual angles.

PANEL 4: AN ANGRIER, MORE CONFIDENT REI

The most important thing now is to change Rei's expression. In the script for panel three, Rei is trying not to act scared, but she's intimidated. In the fourth panel, she gains confidence and is pissed off! In panel three I turned the inner parts of her brow up to hint at her fear. Here she is a full-fledged meanie!

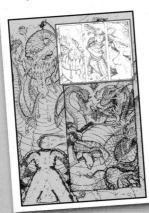

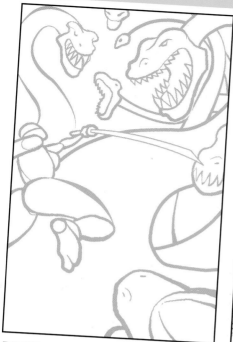

PANEL 5: THE COOL ACTION PANEL!

I chose not to have Rei fill up a lot of the space because there had to be plenty of room to accommodate the dragon and its heads.

In the first panel, you can count eight necks. Here there are seven heads. I figured that after filling up most of the space with heads, leaving one out wasn't going to hurt. I like their size variation and the composition of the necks the way it is.

Speaking of dragonheads, notice that they're all drawn in different angles with varying expressions; redundancy with similar elements sticks out like a sore thumb. I still showcased the main head (from panel 2) facing Rei as if it's the one she's attacking first.

I added curved, loose crosshatching on the necks for scales (to be completed later). The horizontal underbelly scales describe the curvature of the tubelike necks.

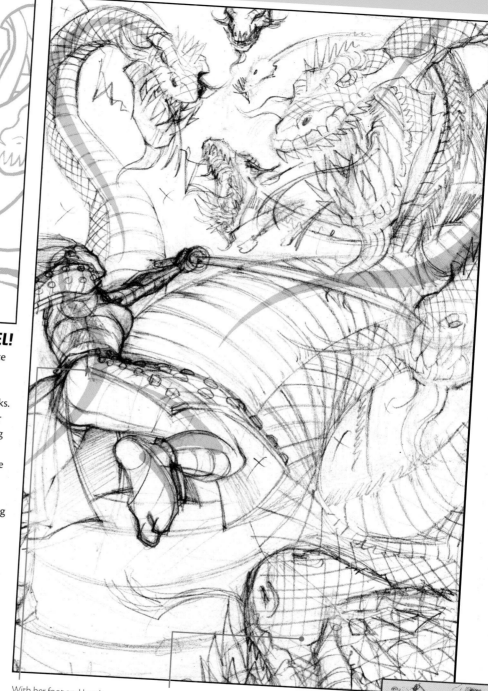

With her foot and legs larger and her upper body smaller, the foreshortening is exaggerated more than in the thumbnail. Better!

I added another dragon head to fill space in the lower-right corner.

TIGHTENING PANEL 1

At this point, everything should be mapped out to your satisfaction. All the kinks, perspective and figures are done! I now have enough groundwork completed that I can begin tightening to prepare for inking. But often this stage is the most tedious as it requires so much detailing and patterning. I'll show you how to create details such as dragon scales and other stylistic features.

Tightening is more or less just a matter of choosing your final lines and darkening them. Of course, because we're working in pencil, nothing is absolutely final yet.

PANEL 1: SMOOTHING OUT

Any changes are usually made to refine elements that didn't look right in the rough: correcting the top contour of the main neck, pulling up the far right tooth for symmetry and lowering the right "cheek beard" (or whatever that is!) for the same reason.

The mountain line and small dragon head way in the back are blacked in, pushing them back so they won't compete with the elements in front. The crosshatching in the background is just to fool kids into thinking there's more detail there. If they think that makes the piece cooler, so be it—as long as it's not interfering with the piece's basic structure (as I've always stressed!).

Instead of picturing Rei completely in silhouette, I've added rim lighting to make her pop. Imagine the bright, flaming dragon drool as a light source in front of her.

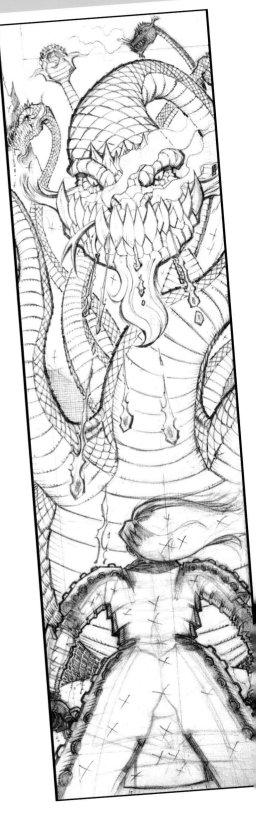

WHAT'S WITH THE X?

An X indicates an area of a penciled piece to be blackened. It beats scribbling in! (If the area is small enough, however, I'll go ahead and scribble.)

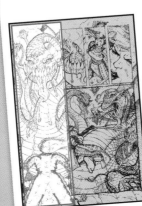

DRAWING SCALES

Here's an easy way to construct scales for a dragon or other reptiles. The long underbelly scales are simple enough to figure out, especially if you've paid attention to drafting the curves to follow the tubelike form of the necks. Just follow those lines! For the smaller scales, begin with some simple crosshatching.

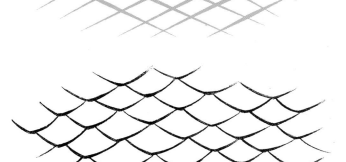

HOW TIGHT DO WE GO?

It depends. You can draw so tightly that your drawing could be printed straight from your pencils (as many of the examples in this book are), or you can leave it a little rough to allow more spontaneity in the inking stage. Many pencillers who ink their own work tend to draw looser; those who work with another inker may draw tighter to provide enough information for an inker.

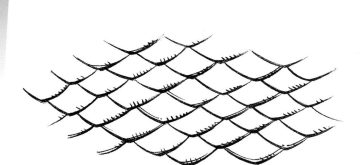

1 ROUGH OUT A CROSSHATCH PATTERN
Crosshatch at an angle to create diamond shapes rather than perfect squares.

2 ROUND THE BOTTOM CORNERS
Round the corners ever so slightly, overlapping them a little past the top corners of the diamond shapes underneath.

3 DARKEN THE UNDERSIDE OF EACH SCALE
Add shading to give dimension. You can even embellish a bit by adding minor hatching to the darkened side of the scales.

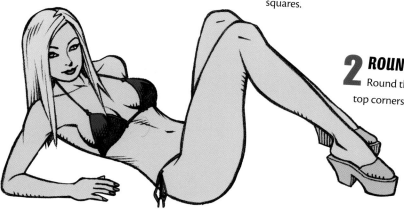

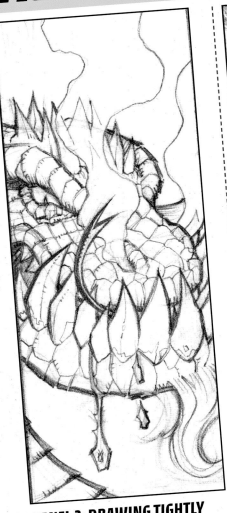

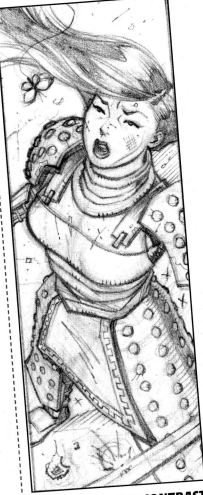

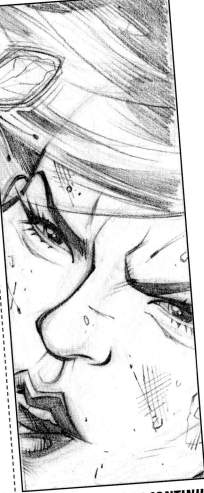

PANEL 2: DRAWING TIGHTLY

The scales on the head don't follow the pattern shown in the demonstration on page 99 because they're different in nature.

I left a minimal amount of detail behind the smoke to make it look somewhat transparent. The thin lines contrast starkly with the thick lines in the contours of the head and neck. I generally draw thick outlines and thin interior lines.

Minding the script (page 91) I gave the dragon an evil smile by curling his upper lip and pushing up the eyelid. Whatever helps, right?

PANEL 3: ADDING CONTRAST AND DIMENSION

I tightened the hair, added highlights and dirtied Rei's face—mostly dots and dashes to indicate charring and soot (as indicated in the script). These light lines will contrast with the bolder features of her face but won't detract from her youthful appearance.

I checked reference photos and made more sense out of the butterfly wings. (without making them look like a monarch's at Keith's request). If I hadn't used a reference, it would have looked like a large fly.

I added dimension via thick, darkened edges on the side of the shoulder clasps, under the cloth belt, and on one side of the knobs on her armor. Scratch and wear marks on her chest add texture. A pattern on her loin cloth and a shiny sparkle off the sword provide the icing!

PANEL 4: MAINTAIN CONTINUITY

Of particular concern here are Rei's Asian eyelids. Check references or see page 101 to draw them accurately.

I've hinted at the butterfly by drawing wings—this time with more detail and "ghost" contour lines to indicate flapping—just enough to tie it to the previous panel, but not too much.

I tend to darken most of the upper lip and the underside of the lower lip (see page 39).

In the ongoing effort to maintain continuity, I mimicked all the little blemishes on Rei's in the same locations in the previous panel.

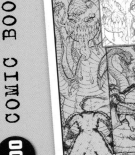

PANEL 5: TOUGH AND SATISFYING

This last panel can be tough for a beginner, but here are some tried-and-true ways to tackle it:

- Work one subject at a time; in this case, one dragon neck at a time.
- Work from foreground (Rei) to background (farthest dragon heads and mountains).
- Start on your favorite elements first, then proceed to your next favorite, and so on.

Rendering scales seemed endless because I treated each individually. Notice how I added shadow areas along the neck of the left dragon. Remember, patience is your friend. Sure, I could've done simple feathering, but it looks cooler to highlight each scale—and I'm all for cool!

I added smoke steaming out of the main dragon head and the one in the lower right in anticipation of an imminent attack. Faint detail behind the smoke keeps it semitransparent.

I've added a scribbly border around this panel and speed lines to suggest swift action. I didn't overdo the jagged border, because technically they aren't fighting yet. The spiral speed lines from the border beat straight lines any day!

NOT COIN SLOTS WITH DOTS!

Two things separate Asian eyes from Western eyes: the absence of eyelid creases (usually) and the epicanthic fold on the inner corner of the eye. This is a web of skin overlapping the lower eyelid at the inside corner. Some Western eyes and mixed-heritage eyes have epicanthic folds, but it's not as common. You can see these folds on Rei, but you can't see eyelid creases.

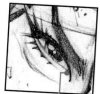

Epicanthic fold

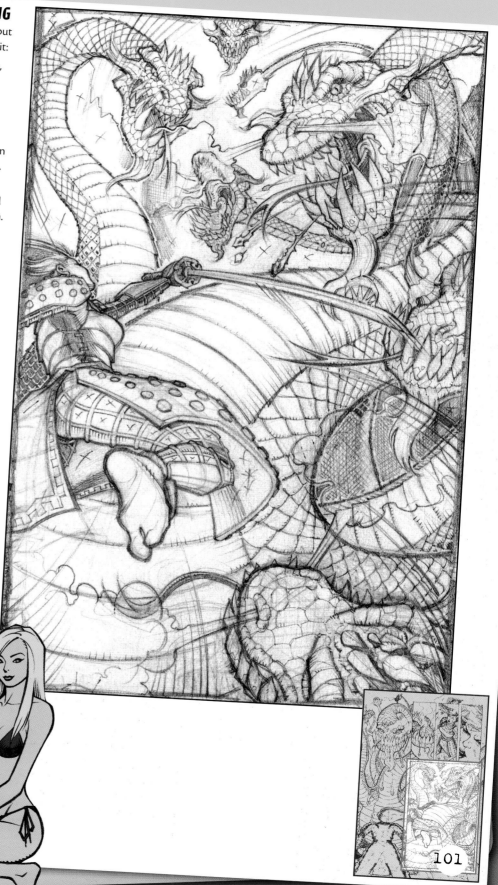

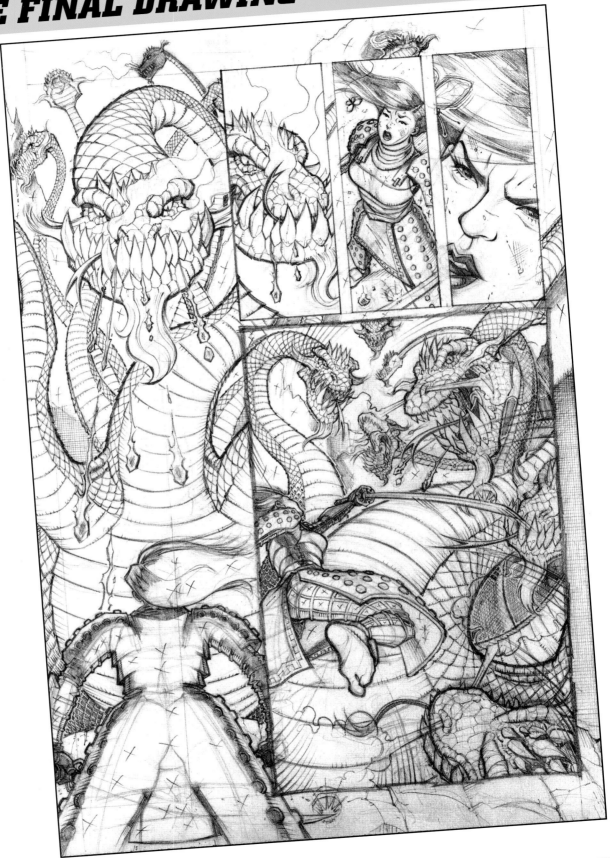

THE BASICS OF INKING

No comic book art is truly finished until it's inked. Technology allows pencil art to be tweaked and printed (as seen in most of this book), but most people prefer the slick definition of ink.

Inking is not tracing. Think of it as polishing and enhancing your pencil sketch as you redraw it. Besides, tracing your pencil art is harder than it seems. You have to learn to separate objects clearly, adding shadows, texture and any details that you've neglected in pencil. Control of your tools is imperative!

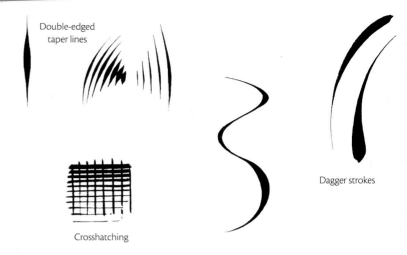

Double-edged taper lines

Dagger strokes

Crosshatching

BRINGING PENCIL TO LIFE

A variety of thick-to-thin and thin-to-thick lines combined with feathering is the key to strong inking. Here, Rei's head displays the these strokes.

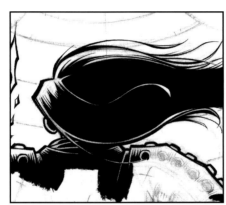

DIFF'RENT STROKES (I KNOW ... I KNOW)

First, master the *dagger stroke:* a line that begins thin and gradually becomes thicker, or vice versa. Learn how to do it both ways. Practice making dagger strokes in curves, too. If you can master this, you can ink.

Also try *double-edged tapers:* lines that are fat in the middle and thin at the ends. Start very thin (your brush tip should just graze the paper) to really fat (apply more pressure) to really thin again (ease off).

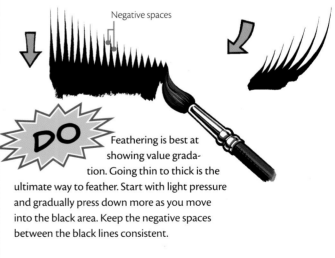

Negative spaces

DO

Feathering is best at showing value gradation. Going thin to thick is the ultimate way to feather. Start with light pressure and gradually press down more as you move into the black area. Keep the negative spaces between the black lines consistent.

THE WORLD OF BRUSH INKING

The most valuable skill in inking is learning how to do it with a brush. If you can master the brush, you can achieve any line faster than you can with a pen, and your line widths and varietals will be endless.

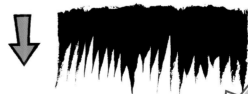

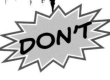

DON'T

Here's a sloppy set of feathering done by swiping lines out from the blacks as if you were shading. This method is too hard to control and can result in an uneven pattern.

103

INKING SPEED LINES

Here's the last panel of our script, showing curved dagger strokes used as dramatic speed lines. The longer lines (as well as the blade of the sword) were done by swiping a pen along a French curve (see page 7). Although I don't recommend using a French curve for every line, it's a handy tool for long, precise lines. Here's how you can imitate an impossibly long, brushlike dagger stroke with a pen and a French curve.

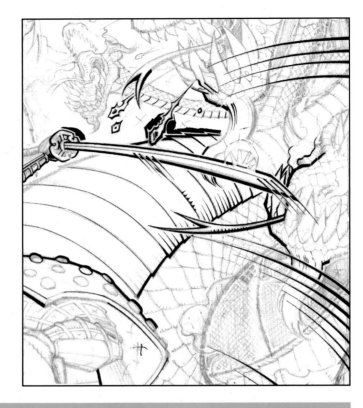

I must stress the need for line variety in your inking. This example is inked badly. It has little life and seems flat. The only thing I can credit this version for is wide contours and thin interior lines.

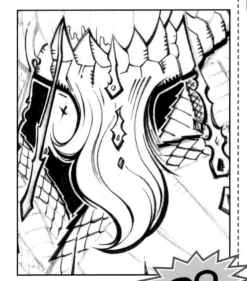

In this partially inked version, you can see everything about inking.
The variety of widths in the lines gives a very animated feel and everything seems to flow. At the very least, it's just cooler to look at, no?

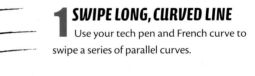

DEMONSTRATION

1 SWIPE LONG, CURVED LINE
Use your tech pen and French curve to swipe a series of parallel curves.

2 SWIPE ANOTHER SET OF LINES UNDERNEATH
Add another curve at a very slight angle under the first, allowing each pair to meet at a pointed tip on one side. Don't overlap; if you do, use fluid correction to get rid of the overlap.

3 FILL IN OUTLINED STROKES WITH BLACK
Voilà! Now you've deceived others into thinking you're a brush-control genius!

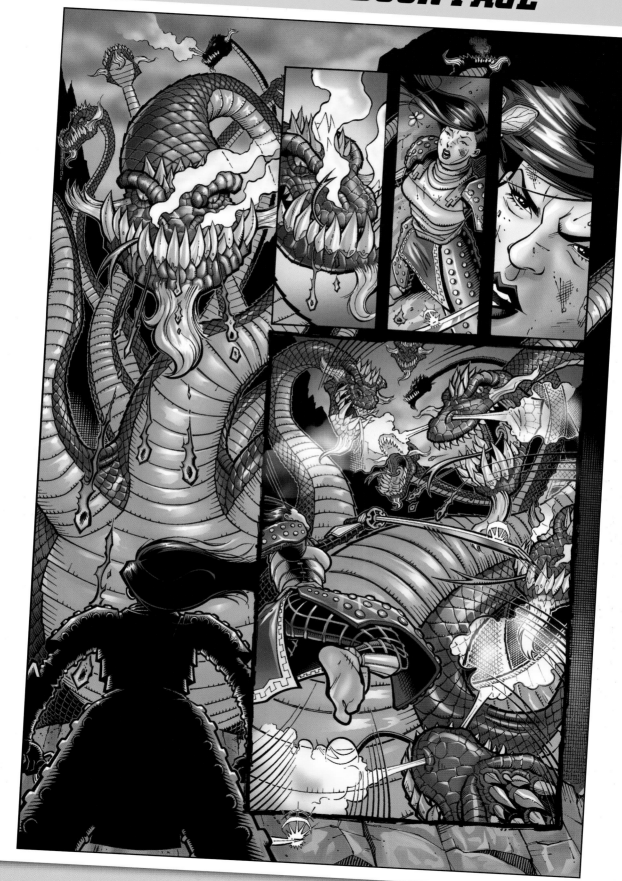

REVIEWING THE SCRIPT

MONICA AND MONTE

Sometimes artists have to work in more restricted or predetermined layouts for their pages. This is most prevalent in comic strips or newspaper-style pages where the panels must be equal size and shape. This restriction requires us to use our composition skills wisely.

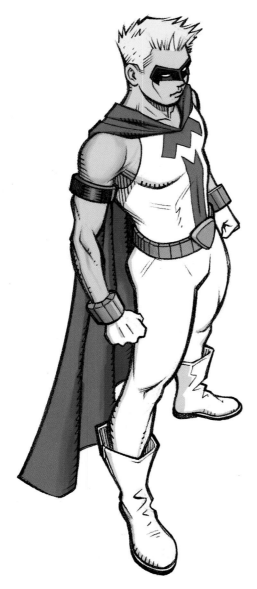
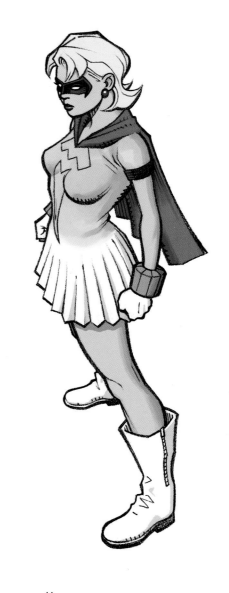

OUR PROTAGONISTS

Monica Mass and her brother Monte are teenage characters that David Watkins and I created in the late 1990s. On the next page is the two-page script for one of the sibling's adventures that Dave handed me for this lesson.

READING THE SCRIPT

For this lesson we'll use a script that requires the artist to work in eight panels spread over two pages. In other words, we have four equal panels (or quadrants) on each page.

MONICA AND MONTE SCRIPT PAGE ONE

PANEL ONE
Monica and Monte Mass hovering outside of cave, actually a hole in a mountain.

Monica: That's it, Dr. Destruckto's hidden lair.

Monte: Doesn't seem all that hidden to me.

Monica: Oh, shut up.

Monte: I'm just sayin'.

PANEL TWO
Monica and Monte fly into the cave. Their eyes are glowing.

Monica: Use your flare vision, Monte.

Monte: I know my own powers, Sis.
Don't nag me.

PANEL THREE
Monica and Monte are confronted by a huge monster in the cave. Any kind of monster.

Monte flies toward the beast.

Monica: Looks like that fiend has a little help.

Monte: Not for long.

Monica: Monte, wait!

PANEL FOUR
Monte is swatted and flies backward into the cave wall.

Monte: Oof!!

Monica: He's too big for us to charge. We need to work together.

MONICA AND MONTE SCRIPT PAGE TWO

PANEL ONE
Monica grabbing a fallen Monte by a foot.

Monica: And I've got just the idea.

PANEL TWO
Like a bat, Monica swings and hits the monster with Monte.

Monica: Batter up!

Monte: Hey!

PANEL THREE
The monster goes down, but Monica flies into his belly for the final blow.

Monica: Sleep tight, Ugly. Don't let the bed bugs bite.

Monte: That was so unnecessary. I'm not a piñata.

PANEL FOUR
The monster is down. Monica is grabbing Monte's hand as they walk toward us deeper into the cave.

Monica: Whatever. C'mon, now let's get that big jerk, Dr. Destruckto.

Monte: I'm hungry.

THUMBNAIL LAYOUTS

As with the comic book-style script, start by sketching thumbnails of how you envision the pages and panels. Having already composed some images in my head as I read the script, I began to lay out what came to mind. These panels read from the top left to right, and then to the bottom left to right. Again, keep it small, simple and quick—a thumbnail is by no means a finished product!

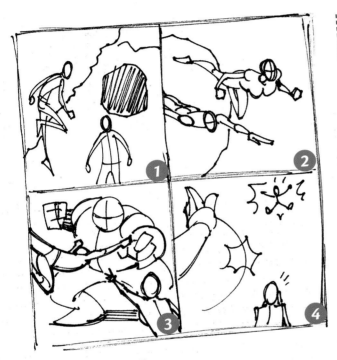

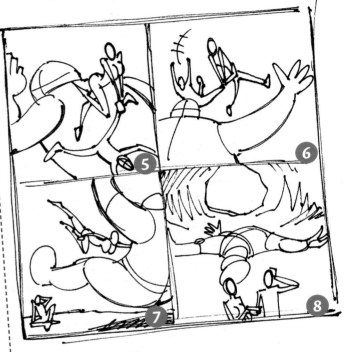

PAGE 1 THUMBNAIL

PANEL 1: An aerial shot, looking right at the hole in the mountain. The characters' backs are to the viewers, but I wasn't sure if this was an effective way to introduce the characters.

PANEL 2: As long as there's "frontal" introduction in the second panel, I'm fine with the first. I may change the angle and direction of the characters, though—I'm just not sure I'm feeling it.

PANEL 3: The monster shot! I wanted to show the monster as if it's so big that it's cramped within the panel's borders. Ultimately, I may have to move Monica away from the monster's crotch!

PANEL 4: A fun panel. I'm trying to capture three things in one image: the swatting motion of the monster's hand, Monte's resulting impact against the rocky wall and Monica's expression of concern. A swift action line and starburst effect show motion and impact; the mind fills in the rest.

PAGE 2 THUMBNAIL

PANEL 5: The most difficult panel. Dave wanted Monica to grab Monte as he's falling, and with limited panels this may take a few stabs. Drawing her holding Monte's leg while in the air will look just like that—holding Monte's leg while in the air. As I'm sketching, I'm trying to think of a better way to show Monte falling when Monica grabs him.

PANEL 6: This is an opportunity to showcase body language and facial expression. My biggest task is to make Monica's swinging body motion believable, using a baseball player's mid-swing for reference.

PANEL 7: Monica's flying punch into the monster's gut. Again, body language is key, as Monica's arched, rigid body gives the impression of strength behind the punch. Monte recovers by rubbing his head.

PANEL 8: Here, the siblings walk toward us for a last look. The vertical composition of the cave opening, the monster in the middleground, and the Masses in front create an interesting perspective, but who knows—I may experiment a little later.

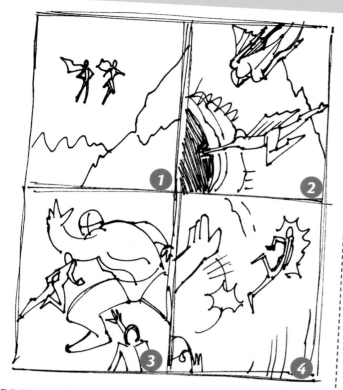

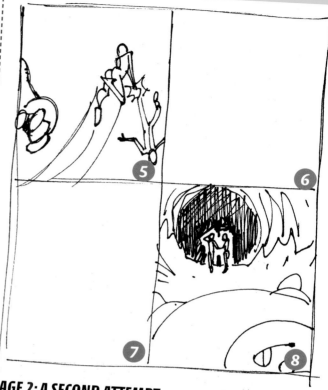

PAGE 1: A SECOND ATTEMPT

PANEL 1: A hint of the big mountain in the foreground, with the siblings floating in the background. Although I wanted a good front view of the pair for the introductory panel, reducing their size to show scale in relation to the mountain took precedence.

PANEL 2: Flipping the angle completely around, we see Monte and Monica flying toward the hole in the mountain that was hinted at in the previous panel. Although angle variety is what we want, we still don't get a clear shot of the characters, so I'm iffy.

PANEL 3: This panel is very similar to the first panel 3, except I brought the monster's hand up as if he were coiling and about to swat Monte (as we'll see in the next panel). I also experimented with Monte's flying pose.

PANEL 4: Again, similar to the first panel 4. Here, I toyed with Monte's body position as it slams against the cave wall. His body is limper and it looks more humorous. I drew Monte smaller and high in the panel, leaving a big "negative" area of the cave wall underneath him. This shows his size and height in the air, and is a good way to lead into the next panel where Monica catches him by his leg.

PAGE 2: A SECOND ATTEMPT

PANEL 5: By drawing the scene from the same angle again, we show time passing within the same space. By drawing Monica catching Monte lower in the panel than he was in the previous panel, we can show that he was in the process of falling. This solves the dilemma! The sequence would have been more effective had both panels been next to each other, but what can you do, eh? The format doesn't allow it ... no biggie.

PANELS 6 AND 7: I felt that the initial sketches of these panels were effective enough to reuse.

PANEL 8: I reversed the vantage point from the first set's final panel. Having the monster in the extreme foreground (and not even showing all of it—perhaps reminding us that it's so big it wouldn't fit in the panel) makes this panel very dynamic. Having Monte and Monica walking in the far background conveys their satisfaction, leaving our readers looking forward to a new adventure.

TWO THUMBNAILS?

Why two different sets of thumbnails? Rarely does an artist hit the mark on the first try. I often rearrange or completely redo panels to tell the story more effectively and enhance the visual flow.

ROUGHING OUT YOUR PANELS: 1ST PAGE

Choose the strongest panels to rough out. Some use tighter thumbnails to make enlargements. My thumbnails are small and sloppy, so I just refer to them and rough straight on the board. You're laying the groundwork for the final rendering, so stay light and erasable.

This sequence has eight equal panels that measure 5" × 4 1/16" (13cm × 10cm). The horizontal GUTTER (the space between panels) is twice as wide as the vertical gutter to cue readers that they should look at the upper panels first. You needn't feel constrained to do this. Feel free to experiment!

Always rough out past the border's edges.

Background mountainscape

Hole in foreground mountain

Diagonal orientation improves the use of space, leaving room for word balloons.

Showing part of the hole with mountains in the background indicates where they're coming from.

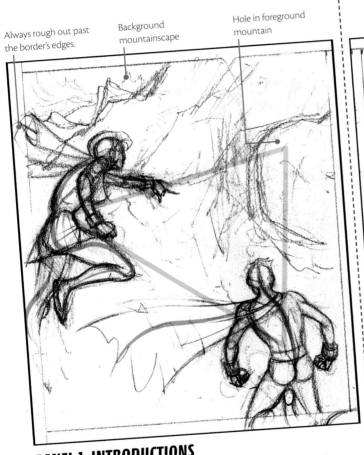

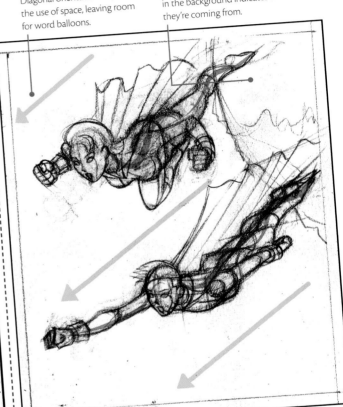

PANEL 1: INTRODUCTIONS

I went with my first thumbnail because I would rather show the characters bigger as we're introducing them. Even though this is a back view, we'll get a chance to see their faces in the next panel.

The triangular composition of the figures and the hole fill out the panel well, while giving a sense of vastness.

Notice how the S-shapes of the lifted capes show that the figures are hovering in the air. S-shapes also emphasize body gestures: elevated elbows and bent legs indicate the need to balance in the air. Focus on developing the shapes of the objects and figures rather than on hard lines.

PANEL 2: ROTATING THE CAMERA

I also chose my first version for panel two so I could show the front of the characters for a good, early look. Besides, it would have been redundant to show the mountain hole again. And, "rotating the camera" always adds interest.

I flipped the thumbnail's orientation so that I now have the pair flying toward the lower-left corner. It's picky, but the direction of their flight will subtly move the viewer's eye toward the third panel when the page is viewed as a whole.

Note the different body gestures, too. The same pose for both panels would have been repetitive.

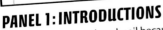

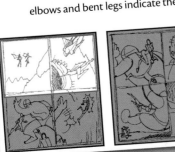

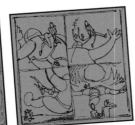

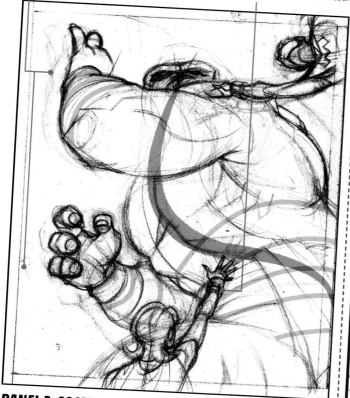

Don't be afraid to move parts around.

Rough out the basic shapes of the muscles before you render.

The bracelets follow the form of the arm here too.

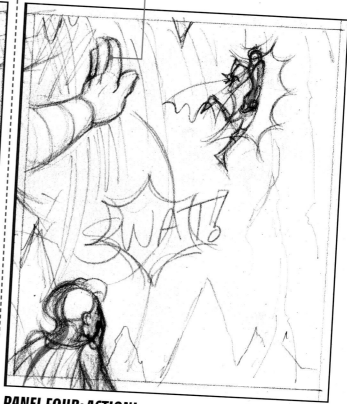

The easiest reference is your own hand (minus one finger!).

PANEL 3: SOMETHING BIG IS ABOUT TO HAPPEN

I went with a slight variation of my second thumbnail because I liked the monster raising his arm before swatting Monte. But instead of drawing the monster straight on, I enlarged and tilted him diagonally and used an upshot angle view. This way, the panel is filled, and the monster appears even larger.

Monica's motion shows that she's saying something to Monte, as indicated in the script. And although the script doesn't say it specifically, the raising of her arm shows her concern for Monte. I even remembered to move her hand from the monster's crotch! Now, Monica's arm moves your eye toward Monte, and his arm and orientation moves it toward the monster—details of composition that work!

Notice the wraps on the monster's forearms; they follow the foreshortened cylindrical form. Also notice the sumo "diapers" curving around his bulky waist.

PANEL FOUR: ACTION!

My second thumbnail worked better. I liked the funnier position of Monte crashing against the wall. The first try was too typical. I had to make him smaller, though.

Remember to rough out past the border's edges. Just because you can't see past the edge in the final drawing doesn't mean that you don't need to establish the whole structure. Also, remember to draw under-structures before you lay anything on top. You can see the basic skull under Monica's hair and Monte's leg and hand even though they're covered by his cape.

I threw in structures erupting from the cave walls at the top and bottom. It beats a flat, boring rock surface. The walls also have been scribbled in to show the cave's direction and curvature.

Finally, I added two starbursts: one showing the past action of Monte getting swatted and one where Monte hits the wall. The starburst, the motion line, the follow-through of the monster's arm and Monte hitting the wall all help the reader understand what has happened. This beats drawing two identical panels; one pre-swat and the second post-swat!

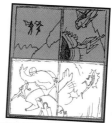

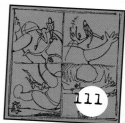

Keep the capes flowing in the direction of the wind.

Action lines following the starbust help imagine Monte's impact site.

Even a simple curve is better than a stiff body.

Use references for the muscle if you're unsure.

Rough the arm and hand beyond the border to place the thumb correctly.

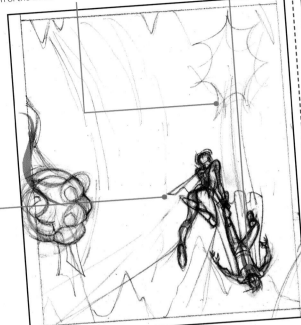

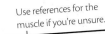

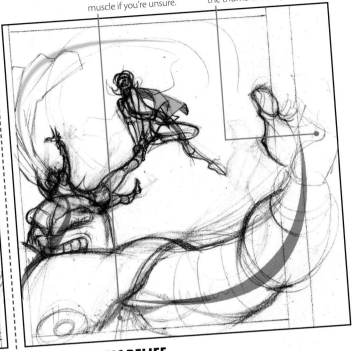

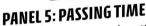

PANEL 5: PASSING TIME

Here's an instance where the setting stays the same, but the characters have moved. I could've tried to combine and cram to depict all of that action in one panel, but it would've been too much. Besides, the script called for this panel, and we must fill eight.

Be sure to maintain the general proportions of the characters from one panel to the next. If they've changed spots, their sizes must be correct in the new locations. Even professional artists can be careless about this, double-check! Maintain the general flow of the cave wall and its jagged edges as well.

Time has passed, and the monster's arm will have moved by the time Monica retrieves Monte by the leg, so I dropped the arm following the swatting. I drew action lines trailing Monica from her original spot in panel 4. Even without those lines, viewers can see that she has flown to catch her brother, but the lines enhance her speed and urgency.

PANEL 6: COMIC RELIEF

This is potentially the funniest panel because of the action and facial expressions. To make the most of it, I need to show three elements:

- Monica in mid-swing as she whips her brother like a baseball bat
- Monte flailing like a rag doll as he strikes the monster
- The monster's reaction to being hit

I cropped the monster because he's the biggest element. I figured that all I had to show were the monster's facial and bodily responses so I could save the rest of the space for the siblings' action. I drew one arm flailing to show his reaction. The composition now brings the characters closer to the eye, drawing more attention to the focal point: the use of Monte as a baseball bat.

Body gestures show action and reaction as well. Having drawn baseball players, I was familiar with what makes an effective mid-swing: the hips and lower body should be well ahead of the upper body and turned in the direction of the swing. Grimacing is a must for Monica as she uses all of her strength to swing her heavy brother—her head is back and her eyes are tight as she shows that extra effort. The monster, of course, is wincing in pain.

CARTOON STRIP: RESTRICTED FORMAT

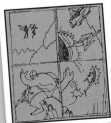

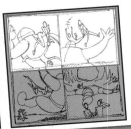

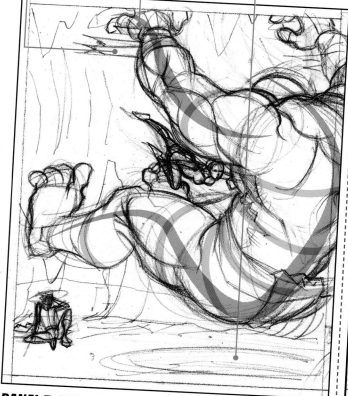

Use loose ribbons to show movement!

Bent fingers and toes show lifelessness, aiding in the depiction of impact.

A shadow prevents the monster from being stuck on the background.

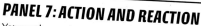

Estimate the height for proper proportion.

Perspective lines follow the diagonal orientation of the monster, leading the siblings to darkness in the top-right corner.

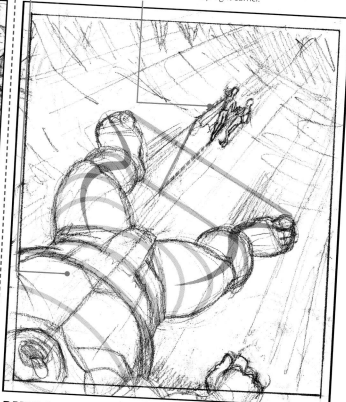

PANEL 7: ACTION AND REACTION

Yet another action panel. Unlike panel 6, I've decided to pull back a bit and show a lot of the monster to avoid redundancy. Now I can maximize his flailing arms and legs as he's being pushed by the force of Monica's flying punch. The reduced size of Monte and Monica won't affect my ability to clearly show their status.

Monica is confidently poised with a clenched fist and one knee up as she rips through the air and plows into our beast. The monster's body is curved to reflect the impact of Monica's punch. Monte, in the background, is seated rubbing his head, looking dazed as he recovers from his previous collision with the monster.

The monster occupies the most space, but notice that he is not right in the center of the panel. Placing a bulky form away from the center not only creates visual interest, but in this panel it also suggests movement within time and space. The empty background on the left side of the panel draws us toward Monica's flying punch at the center.

PANEL 8: TOWARD ANOTHER ADVENTURE

I decided to ditch both initial designs for a brand new perspective. Showing Monte and Monica from the original perspective would allow me to show less of the monster than I wanted to.

This slight downshot not only shows everything, but offers a nice change from straight-on shots. You don't need to show the entire monster to get the point; he's just plain knocked out! Throw in a hanging tongue for humor, and take yet another opportunity to show those ridiculous nipples!

I estimated from previous panels that Monte's height is a little taller than the monster's foot. Always keep the proportions consistent!

My main effort with the siblings was to show them walking away calmly and one leg up does the job. Since they are so small, gesture is most important.

Having gone through such intense action, it's nice to close this strip with a quiet panel. In fact, "bookending" this action-packed strip provides a nice variety.

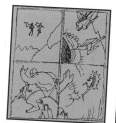
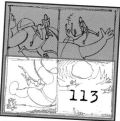

113

TIGHTENING THE PANELS: 1ST PAGE

At this point we'll begin tightening the roughs to prepare them for inking. These two pages will be tightened in the same manner as the comic book page. For each, I will point out specific details that were in my mind throughout the drawing process. All the grunt work is done; now we just have to add details.

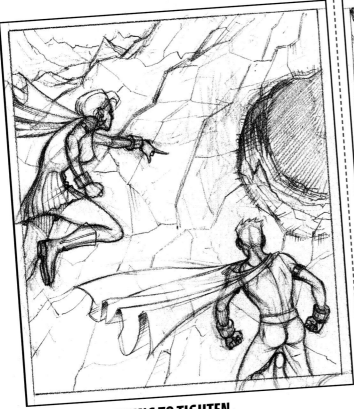

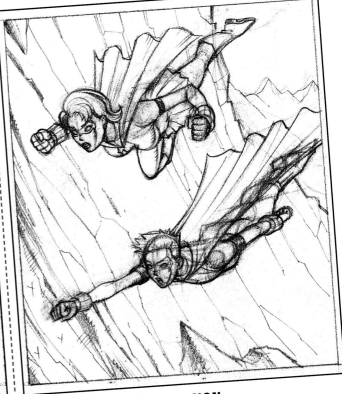

PANEL 1: BEGINNING TO TIGHTEN

Because this was going to be inked, I didn't want to draw every nook in the mountain's texture. Instead, I left enough room for spontaneity. I indicated receding line thickness in the mountains moving farther into the background. This will separate the three planes of mountains a little better; hopefully it will be even clearer after inking.

While tightening, plan black areas for shadows. Here, the obvious choice is the hole. Not only is it dark inside, but the contrast will draw the eye toward the area the siblings are looking at, too. A few lines hatched from the hole will blend it into the mountain.

The most detail is in the accessories, boots, pleated skirt, arm bands and fingers. I scooted Monte's left arm and shoulder in just a touch because it jutted out farther than it should.

PANEL 2: SHOWING DIMENSION

Again, you can see thick lines at the edge of the hole Monte and Monica are flying into. The background mountains only occupy space and thus have fainter lines. The rugged wall texture gets thicker and darker as we move to the lower-left corner, toward which the siblings are flying. The lines are ever-so-slightly curved to give the impression of a round, giant hole. I threw in jagged rocks at the top and bottom—a motif I'll repeat throughout. I also lit the scene to show dimension: one side of the rocks is in darkness, shown with crosshatching, which balances the other side's brightness. I hinted at this lighting effect on the faces as well by adding a separation line.

After roughing out and constructing Monte and Monica's backsides, it is always a little sad to cover them up with their capes!

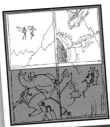

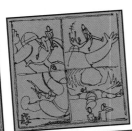

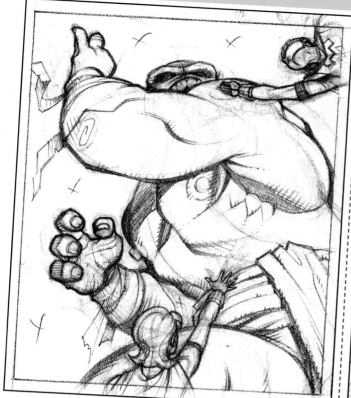

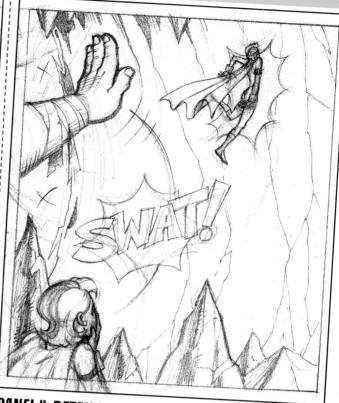

PANEL 3: MINOR ADJUSTMENTS

Most of the changes to this panel are too small for most people to notice. I slightly shaved off the monster's left brow (on our right), repositioned Monte's hand, and just barely foreshortened both of the siblings' outstretched arms.

Using the cylindrical contours of the monster's forearms, I added ragged bands hanging off them. I included additional details such as the huge nipples, the cast shadow from the monster's raised arm, and some crosshatching to define the musculature. I paid special attention to the wrinkles in the palm of the monster's right hand so that it was believable.

It was fine for me to omit the rocky background for in this panel. I made it black to show some darkness and to break up the monotony of the same background. Besides, the composition filled up the space well enough so that squeezing more texture in the background would have been overkill.

PANEL 4: DETAILS AND EFFECTS

I added more details in the monster's fingernails and ribbon strips around the forearm. I repeated the lighting effects for the jagged rocky points. I shortened Monte's legs; they were too long in the roughs. I made proportional adjustments in previous panels, too. Sometimes when I don't look at my own work for a while, I'll come back with a fresh perspective and see new things that need changing. Another trick is to flip your drawing upside-down or look at it in the mirror. Errors you were oblivious to before now stand out more noticeably; take the initiative and correct these mistakes!

I added the sound effect. Usually the artist doesn't do this because the letterer adds the words. But since it's my drawing, I'll do what I want! Just don't do this too often if you're working with a writer, otherwise he or she may get annoyed. I added the extra four vertical "afterimage" lines right underneath the hand simply for style; they add nothing to the effect.

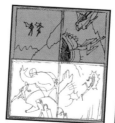

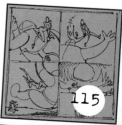

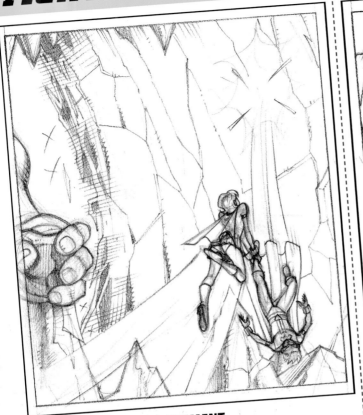

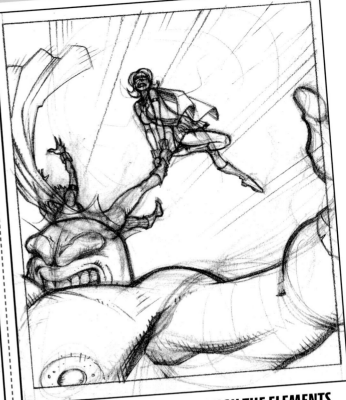

PANEL 5: SHOWING MOVEMENT

Here, I removed the starburst previously roughed in. With two in the last panel, starbursts were getting too repetitive. Too much of a good thing gets old quick and dimishes its value. Also, I prefer the starbursts to define *impact* (pun intended), and putting it here may be confusing. I indicated where Monte had hit with a more subtle, light asterisk.

The detail of the jagged rocks is muted behind Monica's flight trail. I didn't want to show the trail as opaque, but slightly transparent, so I left out some texture to push the rock back. My decision to use a wide flight trail is purely subjective. One could easily use a single swooping line, and perhaps even repeated afterimage lines (although lines may get lost in the background textures).

Finally, Monte's head seemed too small in the roughs, so I made it a little larger to suggest his youth (see page 54!).

PANEL 6: ACTION SPEAKS THROUGH THE ELEMENTS

Here we have the simplest panel in terms of linework and background, but the simplicity of this scene emphasizes the humorous action. The lack of a background provides variety and makes Tommy Nguyen's job easier! I added dramatic speed lines coming from the border toward the collision. The starburst—again indicating impact—made the cut from the rough stage.

I drew some "action hatching" off the end of Monte's cape simply because it looks cool—especially when inked. No need to draw a sweeping action line here unless you really want to. It may actually be overkill since the cape does all the talking.

Other important elements that I retained are the facial expressions: the monster wincing in pain and Monica gritting her teeth (essentially the same expression). A furrowed brow and telling mouth are key.

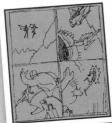

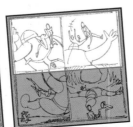

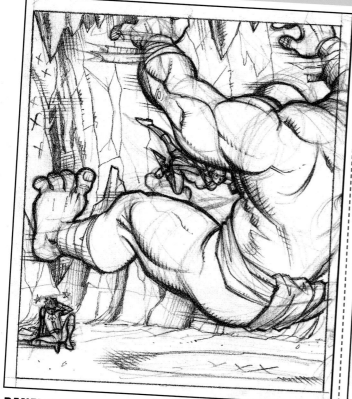

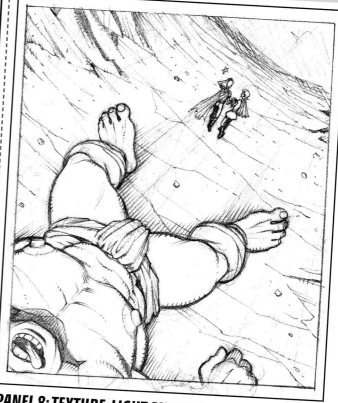

PANEL 7: MINOR DETAILS AND CONTINUITY

My decision to darken the background toward the left side is based on my knowledge of the monster's orientation in the final panel. Since I know that his feet will be pointed toward the darkness of the cave, I thought that this panel should show him facing the same darkness to maintain continuity.

I didn't feel a need to throw an action line trailing Monica since the monster's gesture, arm ribbons and extra speed lines are more than adequate to get the point across. I did not include a starburst where Monica is punching the monster simply because I didn't want to obscure her face.

Other small details that I added are floating stars around Monte's head and some minor crosshatching to soften the edges of the shadow underneath the monster.

PANEL 8: TEXTURE, LIGHT AND WE'RE DONE!

Finally! Keeping the star motif, I threw one next to Monte's head to show that perhaps he's still a bit dazed from his collision with the monster.

If the upper-right corner is dark, it makes sense to have light coming from the lower left. Minimal hatching on the monster's figure should fade toward the light. I put a slight cast shadow under the monster and hatched it with shadow lines away from the light source following the direction of the perspective guidelines. This grounds him so he doesn't appear to be floating!

I didn't do the same with the siblings because they are too small, and they are oriented in the same direction as the perspective lines. So it's no big deal here.

The ground texture gets denser and raised as it curves up at the sides, especially on the left. It gives the feeling of the cave's roundness.

The monster is knocked out, so his muscles are relaxed. Definition should be minimal, especially in the quads of the legs. You can probably visualize where the teardrop muscle goes, but there's no need to delineate every separation here.

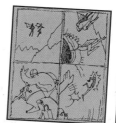

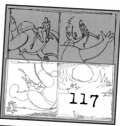

Basics of Inking: THE CROW QUILL PEN

For the story of Rei and the dragon, we learned some inking techniques with a brush. Now we'll talk more about using pens because a lot of the art in the Monica and Monte Mass story deals with smaller figures and textures. Feel free to use whatever technique will work best to get the effect you want.

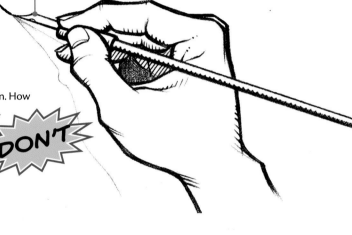

Upside down ... oops!

This is the wrong way to hold a quill pen: it's upside down. How do you tell? The tiny hole in the nib is turned downward. Holding your pen this way not only disrupts the flow of ink, but limits the flexibility of your line width. It's just plain wrong!

DON'T

USING A CROW QUILL PEN

Crow quill pens aren't your typical pens. They come in two parts: the holder and the *nib*, or tip. To use the pen, you dip the nib into India ink. Nib's come in a variety of sizes and degrees of flexibility.

The quill pen's specialty is in very fine lines and dagger strokes. Although stiff enough to help you maintain consistently long, thin lines, these pens also are flexible enough to create some variation in line width. However, they are not as flexible as a brush.

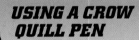

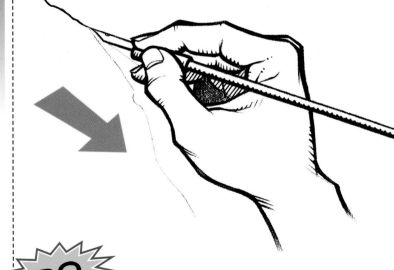

DO

After dipping the pen in ink, touch the tip to the paper so that the hole of the nib is facing up. Pull the pen in the direction of the end of the holder. To make directional changes in your strokes, either rotate the paper or point the end of the holder in a different direction. Remember to keep the nib hole facing up. You'll have the best results if you pull the pen toward you.

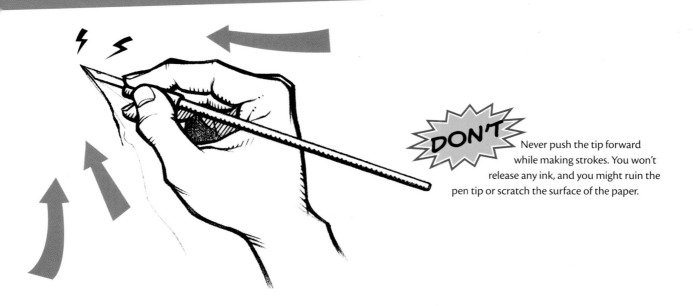

DON'T
Never push the tip forward while making strokes. You won't release any ink, and you might ruin the pen tip or scratch the surface of the paper.

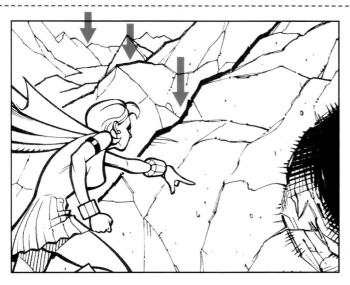

LINE WIDTH TO SHOW DISTANCE

Ah, an inking principle that can't be stressed enough! Here is part of the first panel from our comic strip. Our objective here is to create the illusion of space and distance with the mountains. Because we're dealing with strict black and white, make sure to use wider lines for foreground objects and thinner lines for background objects. Notice how the contours of the mountains get thinner as they recede farther into space. This principle applies to any objects that appear in different planes.

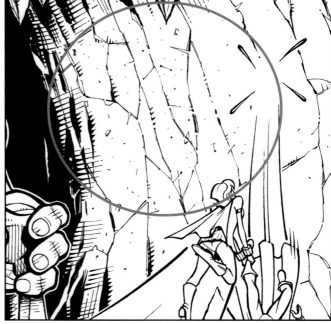

MOUNTAIN TEXTURE

Using a crow quill, I employed a variety of dots and dashes to simulate an irregular surface texture for the rock. There is no formula or drafting involved; just keep it random. You may intensify this texture as it moves away from the light source toward areas of darkness.

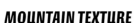

More Inking Tricks: HALOS, HATCHING AND

You may have noticed the use of HALOS (highlighted contours) around people and objects in the "Butterfly Samurai" final inked drawing (page 105). It's a fancy technique used more and more these days by inkers.

Some inkers prefer not to use halos, separating their objects with line widths, contrast and texture. Halos, however, are a foolproof way to keep all your objects separated if you can't or don't know how to do it otherwise. Tim Townsend is a great example of an inker who employs this technique with stunning results and consistency. It's a stylistic choice, tedious to execute; but use it right and it will give your pages that extra pizazz!

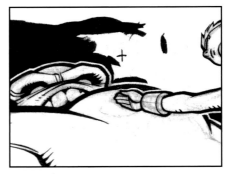

LEAVE WHITE PAPER FOR THE HALOS

In this detail from our strip, we can see that halos can be executed as you go by inking around objects. The contour of a person or object stops short of the contour of the object in front of it, leaving a halo around the nearer object. This example also shows that after the contour of the monster is inked, the black background is inked with a gap between it and the monster, creating a halo. I prefer this method to using white ink (below) .

DEMONSTRATION

ADD HALOS WITH WHITE INK

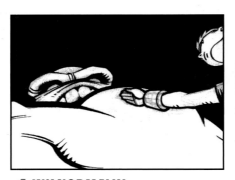

1 INK NORMALLY
Here is another way of creating halos in your inking. First, ink the objects normally, allowing all contours to meet.

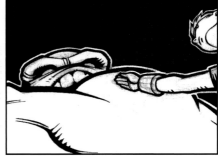

2 OUTLINE WITH WHITE INK
Now, take a brush or pen and dip it into some opaque white ink. Carefully outline the halos around your objects. This may take a bit of practice. It's also difficult to find the right consistency for your white ink. If you must thin your white with water to make it flow easily, you may need several passes to make it opaque enough to cover the black. This is why I prefer leaving white paper for my halos.

120

ACTION LINES

ANGLED CROSSHATCHING

You may notice some fancy crosshatching in the third panel of the first page in the shadow on the monster's chest (holy prepositions!). You'd be surprised at how many people don't know how to achieve this effect. You'd be more surprised to discover how easy it is!

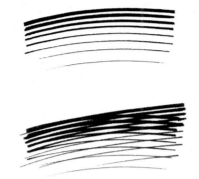

1 DRAW GRADATED LINES

First, do one set of gradated lines (thick to thin). If your lines are very long and you're not confident enough to freehand them, use a straightedge or French curve.

2 OVERLAP AT AN ANGLE

Simply overlap your first set of lines with a second set of gradated lines, crosshatching at a very slight angle—neither parallel to the first set, nor perpendicular.

SWIPED ACTION LINES

In the Butterfly Samurai final inked drawing (page 105), a French curve was used to swipe cool, curved action lines in the final panel. Here, we use straight action lines. With a straightedge with beveled edges (to prevent ink smudging), use your crow quill or technical pen to swipe these lines quickly in order to get that tapered look. You can slicken it up by adding a highlight on the tops of the lines.

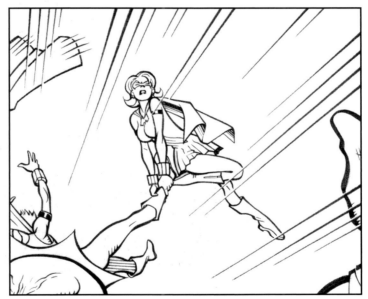

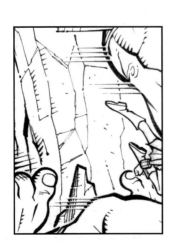

PARALLEL SPEED LINES

Tape down your page and use a T-square to swipe parallel lines quickly and correctly.

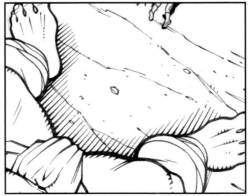

SHORT HATCHES FOR SHADOWS

Here's where it may be more efficient to freehand your lines. I used a small sable brush for maximum control going from thin to thick.

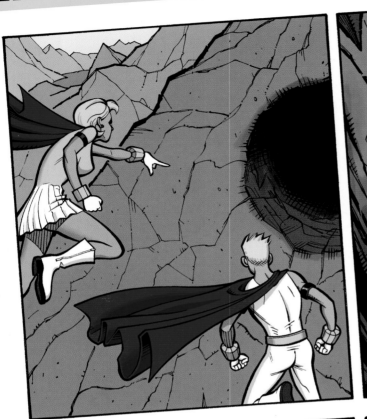

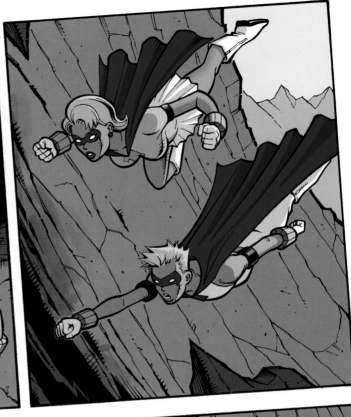

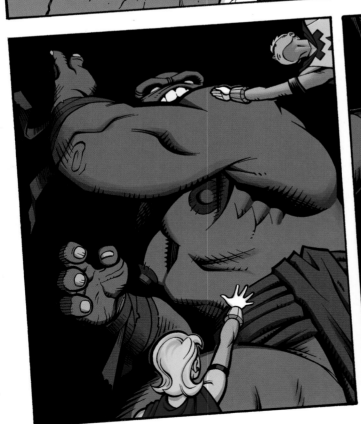

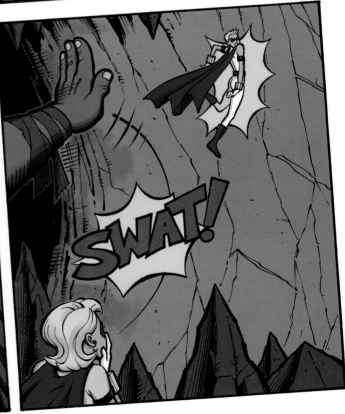

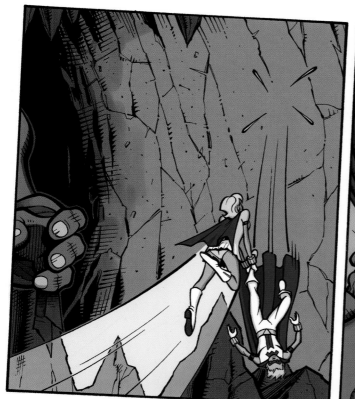

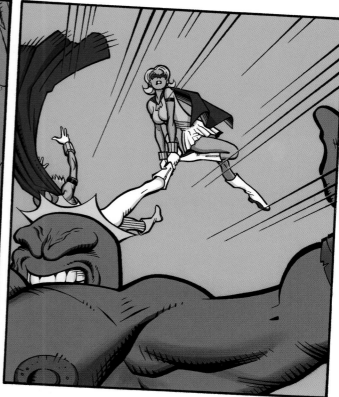

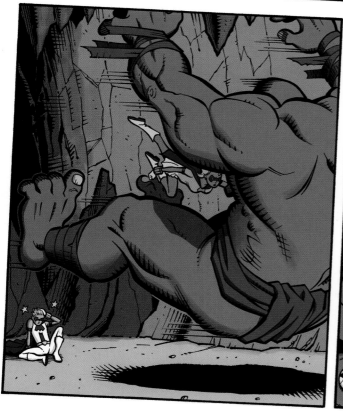

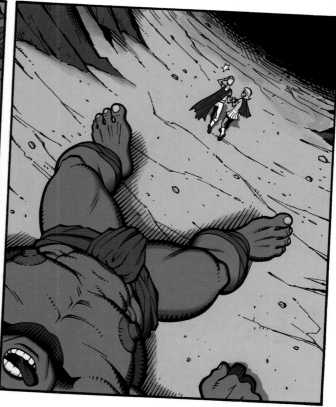

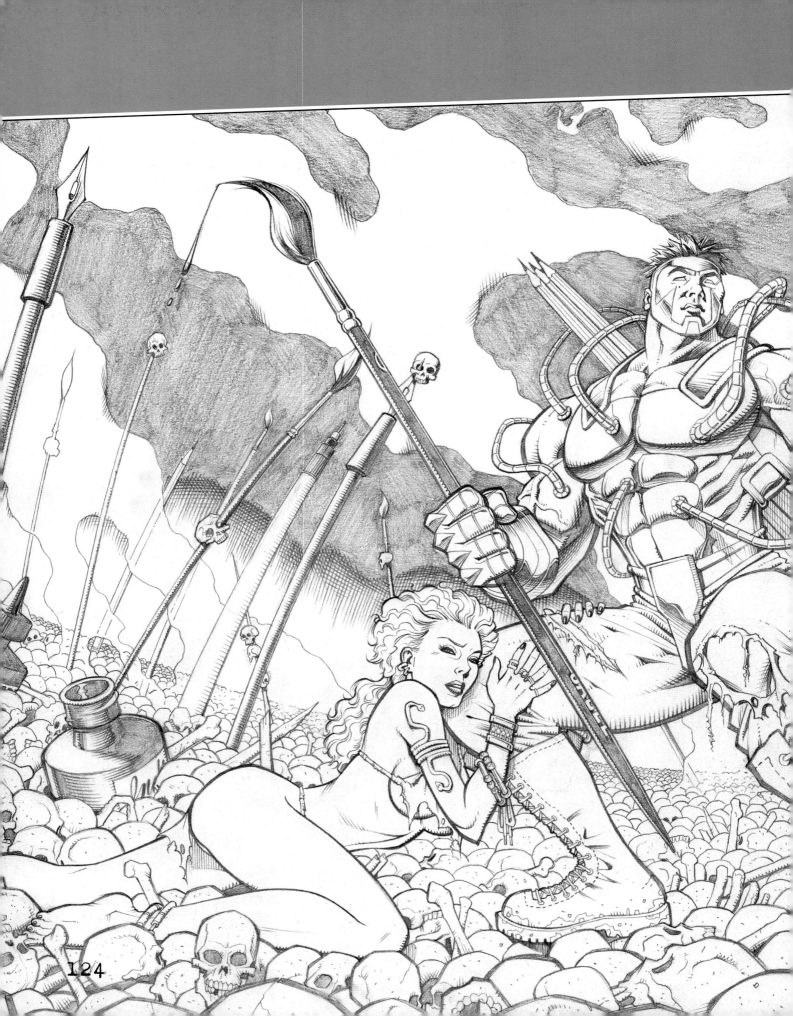

CONCLUSION

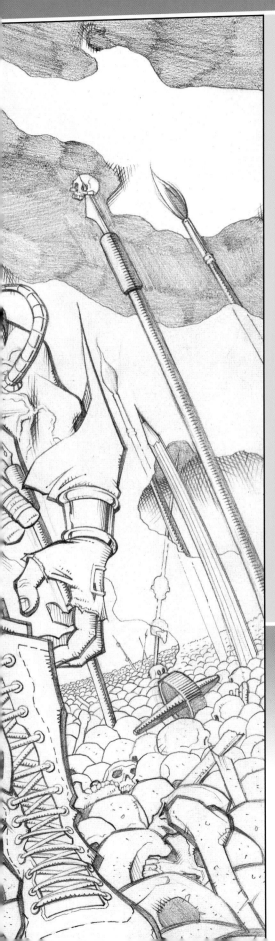

I certainly hope that you got a kick out of this book. More important, I hope you learned something. Although a lot more could have been included, it would've taken more books to explain! You will discover more tricks and techniques on your own as you hone your artistic skills. If you don't get a drawing right, keep practicing. Drawing is like a sport—the more you practice, the better you'll get. Think about it: if you keep throwing a basketball towards the hoop, it will eventually fall right through!

The road to success in the comic book industry is a very rough, competitive one. It helps to get feedback from professional artists and editors to learn what you can do to take your art to the next level (or at least closer). They also can provide valuable information as to what is "in" in comic art as can going to comic book conventions.

Don't let politics or blind editors interfere with your journey; just brush off the worthless stuff and persist. When you are finally ready to submit your portfolio, make sure you focus on pages with sequential art as demonstrated in part 4 "Your Own Kick-Ass Comics." Editors want to make sure you can tell a story. Three to five pages is sufficient. Perhaps add one pinup to round it off. That's it! If you get rejected, don't argue; have a thick skin, take it on the chin and go draw some more.

I wish you success and hope to meet you someday at a show!

Happy Trails!
Tom

P.S.

Oh yeah, don't forget to check out www.TomNguyenArt.com and my DVDs, he-he! Feel free to E-mail me through my site with comments, questions and hate letters.

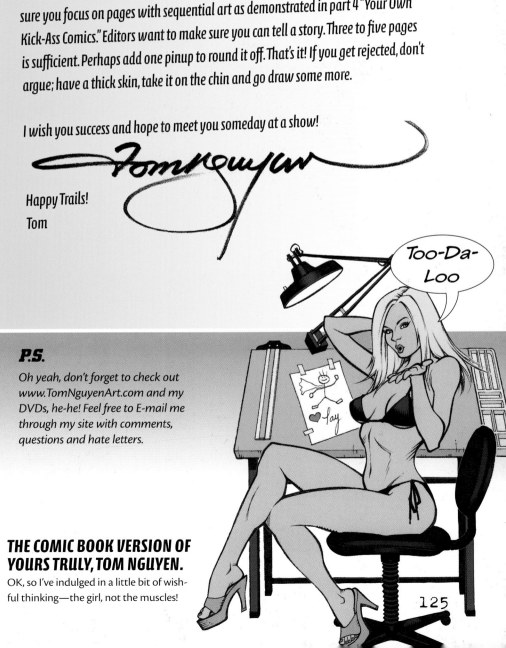

Too-Da-Loo

THE COMIC BOOK VERSION OF YOURS TRULY, TOM NGUYEN.
OK, so I've indulged in a little bit of wishful thinking—the girl, not the muscles!

125

INDEX

IF YOU'RE GOING TO DRAW, DRAW WITH IMPACT!

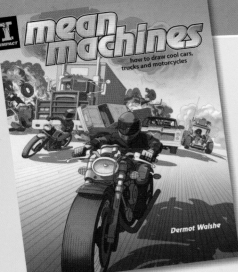

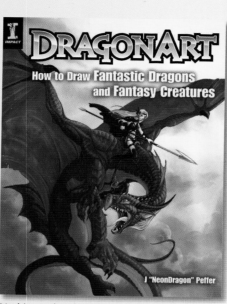

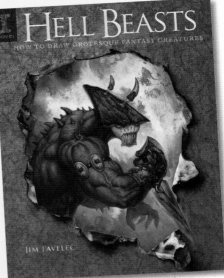

Artists and car lovers alike will love this easy approach to drawing a wide variety of cool cars, trucks and motorcycles. Readers of all skill levels will benefit from the simple beginner techniques for drawing lines and shapes covered in the front of the book, then makr their progress as they work their way through the book to the more intermediate levels. Over twenty demonstrations (each ending with cool finished art) address drawing issues specific to depicting each type of vehicle, including the basic engineering of each different make and model.

ISBN-13: 978-1-58180-828-5
ISBN-10: 1-58180-828-3
paperback, 112 pages, #33504

Nothing makes the imagination catch fire like the dragon, one of the most enduringly popular beasts of legend. Now you can learn simple secrets and tricks for creating your own dragon artworks. Let your imagination soar as you bring majestic dragons and other mythical creatures to life using J. "NeonDragon" Peffer's easy-to-follow progressive line art demonstrations.

ISBN-13: 978-1-58180-657-1
ISBN-10: 1-58180-657-4
paperback, 128 pages, #33252

Let loose the beasts of hell with top gaming artist Jim Pavelec (*Dungeons & Dragons, Magic: The Gathering* and many others). Progressing from the basic to the more intermediate, readers will find everything they need to start drawing a plethora of gruesome creatures. The book covers tools, setup, references and getting started, and features over 25 step-by-step demonstrations for drawing a variety of fearsome beasts including demons, goblins, zombies, gargoyles, hydra and more.

Filled to the teeth with examples and step by steps, and stunning (well, shocking) examples, *Hell Beasts* is sure to teach artists to draw the stuff nightmares are made of.

ISBN-13: 978-1-58180-926-8
ISBN-10: 1-58180-926-3
paperback, 128 pages, #Z0569

Readers will learn to create their own finished graffiti-style artwork beginning with traditional mannequin outlines and shapes and building up to completed, colorful scenes. With step-by-step instruction, Street Scene makes it possible to learn to draw and color everything from faces, figures and clothes to abstract and wild backgrounds.

ISBN-13: 978-1-58180-847-6
ISBN-10: 1-58180-847-X
paperback, 128 pages, #Z0029

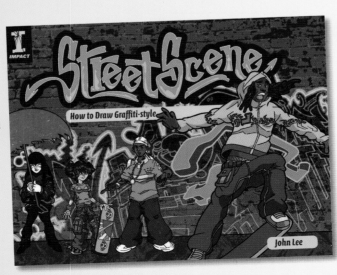

THESE BOOKS AND OTHER TOTALLY AMAZING IMPACT TITLES ARE AVAILABLE AT YOUR LOCAL FINE ART RETAILER OR BOOKSTORE OR FROM ONLINE SUPPLIERS.